Mohawk Region Waterfall Guide

This is the latest in a series of waterfall guides written by Russell Dunn that I recommend to anyone interested in gems which are often overlooked by the public. ... Dunn writes in a lucid style with plenty of historical data and anecdotes which make the guide interesting as just plain reading.

The Long Path North News

Following his successful guides to waterfalls in the Adirondacks, Catskills, and Hudson Valley, Russell Dunn continues with a plethora of falls to explore in the Mohawk region. Again, he does so in a literate, fact-filled fashion with anecdotes and historical data to draw one to these sites.

Adirondac

Catskill Region Waterfall Guide

Dunn's directions are easy to follow, and he offers some nifty history on each of the cataracts. If that's not enough to make you jump in the car, the dramatic photos should cinch it.

Hudson Valley

This book is highly recommended for its unique combination of appealing writing, strong research, intriguing destinations, and interesting history.

Kaatskill Life

Hudson Valley Waterfall Guide

Will very likely open eyes to a world of the outdoors that would have passed us by otherwise.

Times Union

Those who pick up this extraordinary waterfall guide by Russell Dunn will find countless paths to these and other inspirational places in the Valley.

Ned Sullivan, president, Scenic Hudson

Berkshire Region Waterfall Guide

It's a totable package that unveils some hard-to-find springs in the area. Illustrated with historic postcard photos and Dunn's anecdotes, the book is both practical and enjoyable.

Berkshire Living

To our mind, Russell Dunn's regional travel guides are sure to please the outdoor enthusiast on your gift list.

Northeast Antiques

Adirondack Trails with Tales (co-written with Barbara Delaney)

The book stands out from the vast selection of available Adirondack guides by offering a noticeable number of new destinations. ... [But] even when the authors are describing a destination that is relatively familiar, they find a new detail.

Schenectady Daily Gazette

There are lots of Adirondack trail guides. And there are lots of Adirondack history books. But there aren't many books that do both equally well. Licensed guides Russell Dunn and Barbara Delaney have successfully achieved this merger with Adirondack Trails with Tales.

Adirondack Explorer

This is a rich narrative, full of historical nuggets, but still very much a lucid and useful guide for feet on the ground. They have done an outstanding job once again.

Fred LeBrun, Times Union columnist

The breadth and variety of the stories in this compilation distinguish Adirondack Trails with Tales *from other trail guides. ... This wonderful book will better connect visitors and residents with very special places and help them learn from the land.*

Joe Martens, President, Open Space Institute

Trails with Tales: History Hikes through the Capital Region (with Barbara Delaney)

To find such a wide and eclectic variety between the covers of one book, and also within an easy drive of home, is a wonderful gift.

Karl Beard, National Park Service

As a reference tool, it is excellent.

Times Herald-Record

This is a refreshing twist on the traditional guidebook.

Adirondac

Adirondack
Waterfall
Guide

New York's Cool Cascades

Russell Dunn

BLACK DOME

Published by

Black Dome Press Corp.
1011 Route 296
Hensonville, New York 12439
www.blackdomepress.com
Tel: (518) 734-6357

First Edition

Library of Congress Cataloging-in-Publication Data

Dunn, C. Russell.
   Adirondack waterfall guide : New York's cool cascades / by C. Russell Dunn.-- 1st
ed.
      p. cm.
Includes bibliographical references.
   ISBN 1-883789-37-0
   1. Hiking--New York (State)--Adirondack Mountains--Guidebooks. 2.
Waterfalls--New York (State)--Adirondack Mountains--Guidebooks. 3.
Adirondack Mountains (N.Y.)--Guidebooks. I. Title.

   GV199.42.N652A3426 2003
   917.47'53--dc22

                        2003017405

**Outdoor recreational activities are by their very nature potentially
hazardous and contain risk. Please see CAUTION, pg. 18.**

The maps in this book were created using TOPO! Interactive Maps from National
Geographic Maps. To learn more about digital map products from National
Geographic Maps, please visit www.nationalgeographic.com/topo

Cover photograph: "Mossy Cascade," by Nahan Farb, © Nathan Farb
Cover Design by Toelke Associates

Printed in the USA

10   9   8   7   6   5

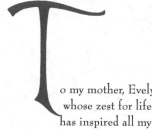

o my mother, Evelyn M. Dunn,
whose zest for life and love of nature
has inspired all my adventures.

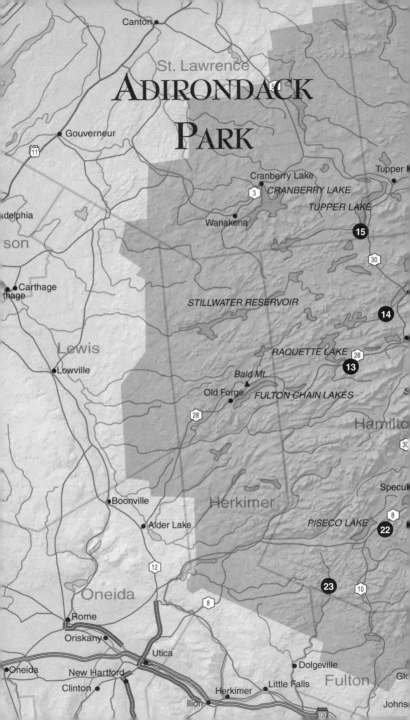

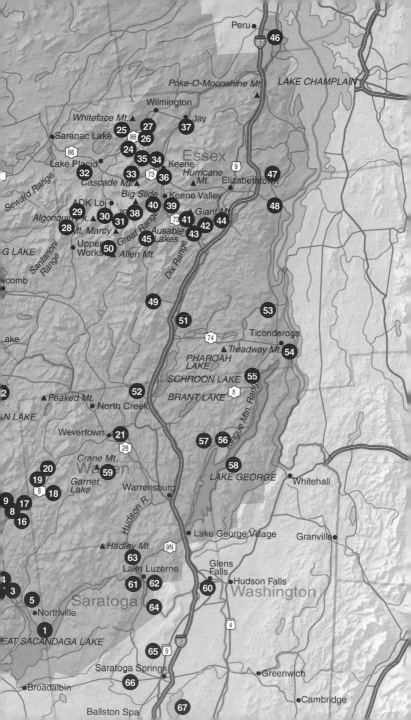

KEY TO MAP

WATERFALLS ALONG ROUTE 30
1. Beecher Creek Falls
2. West Stony Creek Falls
3. Falls along River Road
4. Falls on Groff Creek
5. Tenant Creek Falls
6. Falls on West Branch of the Sacandaga River
7. Cold Brook Falls
8. Auger Falls
9. Austin Falls
10. Whisky Brook Falls
11. Dug Mountain Falls
12. Squaw Brook Falls
13. Death Falls
14. Buttermilk Falls
15. Bog River Falls
16. East Jimmy Creek Falls
17. Griffin Falls
18. Falls on Oregon Trail
19. Shanty Brook Falls
20. Square Falls
21. Dunkley Falls
22. Falls near outlet to Buckhorn Lake
23. Potholers

FALLS ALONG ROUTE 73
24. Monument Falls
25. High Falls
26. Falls at Wilmington Notch Campgrounds
27. Flume Falls
28. Rocky Falls
29. Cascade on trail to Algonquin Peak
30. Indian Falls
31. Falls on tributary to Lake Colden
32. Wanika Falls
33. Cascade Lake Falls
34. Clifford Falls
35. Falls on tributary to Nichols Brook
36. Hulls Falls
37. Falls at Jay
38. Bushnell Falls
39. Mossy Cascade Brook Falls
40. Deer Brook Falls
41. Roaring Brook Falls
42. Falls on North Fork of the Boquet #1
43. Falls on North Fork of the Boquet #2
44. Split Rock Falls
45. Falls along East Branch of the Ausable River
  Pyramid Falls
  Wedge Brook Falls
  Beaver Meadow Falls
  Rainbow Falls
  Artists Falls
  Fairy Ladder Falls

FALLS ALONG I-87 (ADIRONDACK NORTHWAY)
46. Rainbow Falls
47. Falls at Wadhams
48. Falls on Hoisington Brook
49. Blue Ridge Falls
50. Hanging Spear Falls
51. Schroon Falls
52. Falls at Natural Stone Bridge & Caves
53. Stair Falls
54. LaChute Falls
55. Falls on Hague Brook
56. Falls near Clay Meadow
57. Falls on Northwest Bay Brook
58. Shelving Rock Falls
59. Cascade on Crane Mountain
60. Glens Falls
61. Rockwell Falls
62. Mill Park Falls
63. Bear Slide (Buttermilk Falls)
64. Palmer Falls
65. Falls on Snook Kill
66. Rock City Falls
67. Falls on Mill Branch

TABLE OF CONTENTS

ACKNOWLEDGMENTS

First and foremost, I thank my wife, Barbara Delaney, who accompanied me on many of the waterfall hikes described and provided much assistance in putting this book together. Others who have been instrumental include Carl Blazejewski, postcard & stamp dealer at B-Trading Company in Albany, and Robert Drew, postcard collector extraordinaire, for helping me obtain some of the beautiful Adirondack waterfall postcards that accompany this text; Matthew & Catherine Canavan for providing technical support when my computer didn't perform as required; Warren Broderick and Steve Young, local waterfall experts, for their support and for sharing their love of waterfalls; and Trails End in Keene Valley, New York, and West Mountain Inn in West Arlington, Vermont, for their gracious accommodations during our waterfall forays.

The maps were created by Barbara Delaney using TOPO! software. All postcard illustrations are from the collection of C. Russell Dunn. The riddle from *Lateral Thinking Puzzles* by Paul Sloan was reprinted in this book with the permission of Sterling Publishing Co., Inc. All line art illustrations are courtesy of Robert Joki.

I am indebted to proofreaders Matina Billias, Bill Ingersoll, Erin Mulligan, Fred Shroeder, Ralph Keating and Ed Volmar for their helpful suggestions and astute criticisms, and I specially thank Bill Ingersoll for gracing my book with such a well-crafted foreword, and Timothy J. Hallock from the Spatial Information Technology Center, Fulton-Montgomery College in Johnstown for the map of the Adirondack Park.

I am honored to have premier Adirondack photographer Nathan Farb participate in this book by allowing us to use his photograph of Mossy Cascade on the cover.

FOREWORD

One cold winter, on a bleak day in late March that could just as well have been a day in late January, I was snowshoeing with two friends up a frozen stream in the West Canada Lake Wilderness. The season had been so cold the stream was like a frozen boulevard through the woods, with ice several feet thick. Our destination was a remote pond near its headwaters, and the topographic map suggested that the stream would merely be a convenient route to guide us there, nothing more.

We were forced to find a detour, however, when our "boulevard" turned vertical. Although there was not much to see on that particular day, I knew that there was underneath this column of ice a waterfall not shown on any map—one that none of us had expected to find. Nor did we expect to find a second waterfall less than half a mile upstream. Late that spring, when the ice was long gone, and when even the black flies were beginning to fade away for the year, I returned to the area to see the two falls in their liquid state. The stream dropped a combined 120 feet, with the water spreading like white latticework over the final, vertical drop.

I thrill at the discovery of a wall of splashing water and dripping mosses, where an Adirondack stream takes a sudden, rocky step closer to its final destination. I can sit beside a secluded cascade for hours, with the constant sound of rushing water drowning out all concern for the workaday world. When I camp near a waterfall, its sound sometimes incorporates itself into my dreams, reappearing to me in unexpected ways. If I come across a waterfall that I had never known of previously, then it truly is a discovery that I can claim as my own, regardless of whether someone else has been there before me or not. It is the *experience* of discovering the unexpected that I treasure most about Adirondack waterfalls, and the fact that there are still such places to "discover" in New York Sate in the twenty-first century is no small thing.

Russell Dunn has herein compiled a list of some of *his* favorite "discoveries": waterfalls near some of the Adirondack Park's major highways and scenic back roads that for the most part can be found without too much difficulty. Within this book are directions to Fairy Ladder Falls, one of the High Peaks' most distinctive cascades, and the West Branch Sacandaga River, which flows through one of the southern Adirondacks' most inscrutable gorges.

A few of the sites he has selected require some backwoods expertise to reach, but several others are located along the roadsides. These latter often offer insights into the early settlement and industrial development of the region. Overall, Mr. Dunn's list may not exactly coincide with the list I would compile were our roles reversed, but then this is the point. I have found on *his* list quite a few sites that I had never heard of myself, or have not yet had the chance to visit. I can now see that my spring hiking will not be dull for some years to come.

I am pleased to introduce Russell Dunn's *Adirondack Waterfall Guide*, and I expect that his straightforward directions will help not only newcomers to the Park find some of the region's most scenic features, but even some of us who think we *already* know a thing or two about the Adirondacks. I know where I will be next April. Let the pages of this book guide you to many a cascading mountain stream as well.

Bill Ingersoll
South Trenton, New York
July 2003

Bill Ingersoll is the Wild Lands Stewardship Chair for the Adirondack Mountain Club Conservation Committee. He has published articles in Adirondack Life *and* Adirondack Explorer, *and is a monthly contributor to* Adirondack Sports *and* Fitness. *Since 2000 he has been working with Barbara McMartin in updating and reprinting the* Discover the Adirondacks *series of hiking guidebooks.*

INTRODUCTION

Cooling their heels, these youngsters beat the heat on a long ago,
Adirondack summer day.

People have always viewed waterfalls with awe and reverence.
Waterfalls are magical, improbable wonders of nature, leaping
and writhing like tornadoes of frothing white beneath towering
ledges of rock. Their constantly changing surfaces mesmerize like
a hypnotist's disk, and their thundering cry is the voice of nature
incarnate.

Adirondack Waterfall Guide offers a collection of hikes and
drives to waterfalls in the eastern central Adirondack Mountains.
It is a tour of the tiny and the gigantic; of waterfalls located in the
wild, and of those in urban centers; of falls that are heavily visited and those that are unknown save to a few. In compiling this
collection, no attempt has been made to be encyclopedic. There

are simply far too many streams and creeks in the Adirondacks, each containing its own secret glen or cascade, for a book of this size to be comprehensive; furthermore, many waterfalls are on private lands, and thus not readily accessible to the public. But with over seventy accessible waterfalls described herein, some of which are even canoe-accessible, the reader should have no difficulty in finding a suitable cascade to visit.

The waterfall treks described in this book are laid out in the shape of a bracket, with Rt. 30 leading north, Rt. 73 going east, and I-87 (the Adirondack Northway) returning south. It is a journey that will take the reader past major mountain peaks, through what tourism marketers call the "Tri-lakes Region" (Tupper Lake, Saranac Lake, and Lake Placid), and back down the Northway to the Capital Region.

The Adirondacks are uncommonly rich in waterfalls. Just south is the junction of two major river valley systems—the Hudson River, running north to south, and the Mohawk River, running west to east—a geographical feature that has always served as a magnet for attracting settlers, from the first Native Americans to the European colonists. The Adirondacks serve as an enormous watershed feeding the numerous tributaries that descend into the two valley systems.

The Adirondacks consist of an immense tract of land—more than 9,475 square miles, which is larger than Yosemite and Yellowstone National Parks combined and nearly the size of the State of Vermont. The Adirondacks contain 42 peaks exceeding 4,000 feet in height, including Mt. Marcy, at 5,344 feet the highest point in New York State. There are nearly 3,000 lakes and ponds, and over 20,000 miles of streams. With such an enormous mountainous region to collect winter's snowfall, and so many streams to gather and carry water during spring's mighty rush of snow melt, it should come as no surprise that the Adirondacks have an impressive number of waterfalls of various size, configuration, and height.

The Adirondack Mountains are ancient, formed primarily out of anorthosite, an intrusive igneous rock. These rocks are over 1.1 billion years old, making them some of the oldest found anywhere on the planet. After the rocks were formed, they were buried under beds of sedimentary rock miles deep. Later, tectonic forces buckled the region and raised the lands up to a height surpassing that of the present day Himalayan Mountains. Over eons, wind, rain, ice, and snow wore these once-mighty mountains down to a stubble. In the process, the sedimentary rock was removed, exposing the more erosion-resistant anorthosite that presently constitutes the Adirondacks. The waterfalls that we see today are no doubt but a shadow of gigantic cataracts that once must have existed in the early Adirondack days.

WATERFALLS AND BRIDGES

The first thing one is likely to notice is that a significant number of waterfalls in mid-eastern New York, including the Adirondacks, are located next to roads or bridges, and one may wonder why. The answer lies in how cities and villages originally formed in the northeastern United States. During the early days of the Industrial Revolution, a tremendous need arose to harness a steady and reliable source of power to run mills and factories. Waterfalls were readily available as a supplier of energy that was renewable, non-polluting, and abundant. As a result, mills were built next to waterfalls; bridges and roads soon followed; then houses, so that

Many waterfalls have been harnessed for industrial purposes.

Countless waterfalls, like Style Falls, are not readily accessible to the public.

workers would be close to the mills. Finally, whole communities and cities formed—all with waterfalls as their nucleus.

When alternate forms of energy became available in the early 1900s, reliance on hydropower declined, and with it the proliferation of factories and mills along the major and secondary rivers of mid-eastern New York State. One by one, these industries were abandoned and left unattended. Exposed to the relentless, erosive assault of wind and water, they slowly crumbled to the ground, leaving the waterfalls and a smattering of stone walls and scattered bricks beside the roads and bridges. Today, the roads and bridges are a mixed blessing. While they enable one to get to the falls expeditiously, their very presence often compromises the esthetics of viewing the waterfall.

ENDLESS VARIATIONS

Waterfalls come in an endless variety of shapes and sizes. There are towering waterfalls, such as Roaring Brook Falls in St. Huberts, or Rainbow Falls in the Ausable Mountain Reserve; chasm-created falls, such as Ausable Chasm at Keesville, or Flume Falls near Wilmington; broad, hulking cataracts, like Hulls Falls in Keene, or the Falls at Wilmington Notch Campgrounds; falls composed of descending ledges, such as Fairy Ladder Falls near Keene Valley, or Beecher Creek Falls at Edinburg; and falls that form enormous water slides, like Austin Falls near Wells, or Bear Slide near Lake Luzerne.

WHEN TO VISIT

Each waterfall is not only unique—different from all other waterfalls—but also different in itself, depending upon the time of year. Generally, snow and ice persist in their gorges until late April or early May, making access more difficult and dangerous, with the surrounding forest still bare and austere. Spring is the best time for waterfall viewing because all the falls are running at full throttle and guaranteed to put on quite a show. In early spring visibility also is at its peak since there are no leaves on the trees to obscure the view.

In the summer, by contrast, waterfalls turn sluggish and become mere trickles except after a cloudburst unless they are located on major rivers or streams draining substantial watersheds. Huge areas of bedrock and ledges are exposed, and the falls are mere entities of rock, with little water flowing over their rocky mantles. Visibility during the summer is impaired by dense underbrush and tree foliage. There are also the inevitable flies and mosquitoes that tend to collect where the water is stagnant and the underbrush is lush. On the plus side, however, summer does provide a splendid opportunity to jump into the swimming holes found at the bases of many waterfalls.

In the autumn, waterfalls once again become more powerful as rainfall increases, and a burst of glorious colors makes for beautiful waterfall photos. There is also a marked reduction in pesky, biting insects. On the downside, visibility may still be a problem until the trees shed their leaves, clearing the way again for unobstructed views.

In winter, the falls turn to ice or become lost under mounds of drifting snow. Very little rock or water can be observed, and for the duration of many months, waterfalls become virtually indistinguishable from the surrounding cliffs and hillside. Winter is not a particularly good season for visiting waterfalls unless one is an ice climber or visiting an exceptionally large waterfall.

HOW BEST TO VIEW A WATERFALL

As a general rule, the best view is obtained downstream from the waterfall's base, looking directly up at the falls—not from its top. Roaring Brook Falls is a perfect example. If one stands at its top, one will find oneself rewarded with unparalleled views of the High Peaks and the valley below, but one will see little of the fall itself. At best, one may walk away with a general sense of the waterfall's height. To see Roaring Brook Falls in its full majesty, one needs to stand at its base and gaze up. That is when your mouth will drop open and you will whisper, "Wow!" This is true for nearly all of the falls listed in this guidebook.

The problem, however, is that it is not always possible to hike in to the base of a waterfall or climb down from its top. The cataract

T-Lake Falls is the highest waterfall in the Adirondacks and one of the highest in all of New York State.

may be located in a deep gorge with walls so precipitous that descent is dangerous or impossible, or the surrounding land may be private and posted, thus preventing entry. In these instances, a view from the summit of the falls or from the rim of the gorge may be the best that one can do. It may be possible, depending on the terrain, to climb partially down the side of a ravine to view a waterfall from mid-way, which can provide a satisfactory, compromise view.

THE ALLURE OF WATERFALLS

What is it that makes waterfalls so appealing to young and old, to couch potatoes as well as outdoor enthusiasts? Take any other adventure-oriented activity—mountain climbing, caving, white water canoeing, mountain biking, etc.—and you will find that most of the population has no interest in it whatsoever. But the appeal of waterfalls is universal.

The reason may lie within waterfalls' multi-faceted personalities. Waterfalls represent nature at its most sublime—beautiful and captivating on the one hand, yet awe-inspiring and terrifying. When we visit a mighty cataract, we stand spellbound as we watch death dancing on the rocks before us.

We are lured to waterfalls by their thunderous roar in early spring, like a call of the wild. Standing before such power and majesty is exhilarating.

In the summer, waterfalls reveal an entirely different side of their personality, and we are drawn to them by their soul-soothing, gentle patter and babbling as tiny streams and rivulets of water cascade onto the rocks below.

Waterfalls provide a window into the underlying chaotic structure of nature. We watch the endless pattern of falling water, and never see it repeated.

It may be that waterfalls, like thunderstorms, bring about feelings of well-being because of the negative ions released.

But whatever the answer is, we are and will always be drawn to the mystique and majesty of waterfalls.

WATERFALLS AS A COMMODITY

Since early on, the falling waters of streams and rivers have been harnessed to turn waterwheels and turbines in order to generate mechanical and hydroelectric power. Although waterfalls lost favor as an energy source in the early 1900s, a significant number of hydroelectric plants survived in the region and are still generating power today. The demand for hydroelectric power likely will increase in the future as the supply of fossil fuels diminishes; waterfalls— natural or dam-created—provide a readily available, non-polluting, and renewable source of energy.

But power generation is not the only commercial use for waterfalls. They also have been used by hotels and mountain houses to attract tourists, such as at Shelving Rock Falls at Lake George, and High Falls Gorge near Lake Placid. In the case of Krystal Falls in Glenville, and Teepee Falls in Amsterdam, they have even provided the background ambiance for leisurely dining.

Waterfalls have been exploited by exhibitionists wanting to make a name for themselves. At Cohoes Falls, south of the Adirondacks, a daredevil in a barrel went over the 65-foot-high cataract not once, but twice.

Waterfalls have figured in the legends and literature of the region. In James Fenimore Cooper's classic novel, *The Last of the Mohicans*, Hawkeye and his companions sought refuge in Cooper's Cave below Glens Falls to evade a party of Huron warriors, and legend has it that Timothy Murphy, a famous eighteenth-century Indian fighter, once hid behind Bouck Falls on Panther Creek (near Middleburgh) in order to elude a band of pursuing Indians.

WHAT IS A WATERFALL?

There is no commonly-agreed-upon definition as to what constitutes a waterfall. In Bruce & Doreen Bolnick's book, *Waterfalls of the White Mountains*, general guidelines are offered, but these are, at best, arbitrary. According to the Bolnicks, a waterfall is considered to be a single vertical drop of some height; a cataract is a waterfall with a powerful current; and a cascade is a small waterfall, usually containing a series of drops.

Scott A. Ensminger & Douglas K. Bassett, in *A Waterfall Guide to Letchworth State Park,* include a glossary of waterfall terms and define a waterfall as "any sudden descent of a stream over a very steep slope or precipice in its stream bed. Characterized by the stream dropping vertically, or very nearly so. The water must drop a minimum of five feet to be considered a true waterfall." They define a cataract as a waterfall containing a very large volume of water, often falling through a narrow gorge, and a cascade as a waterfall with a very steeply sloped stream bed or a series of small, individual drops.

Rich and Sue Freeman, in *200 Waterfalls of Central & Western New York,* concur with Ensminger's and Bassett's definitions, but also admit that there really are no hard and fast guidelines. There are too many variables to allow for easy categorization. A waterfall may be segmented, fanned, parallel, tiered, serial, plunging, washboard, horse-tailed, terraced, ribbon-like, classical, curtain-shaped, or composed of ledges.

HEIGHTS OF WATERFALLS

Bear in mind that all the heights listed in this guidebook, unless stated precisely, are crude approximations typically made under less than ideal circumstances.

Even with proper equipment, measuring waterfalls can be a tricky business with a certain degree of subjectivity entering the picture. Does one measure a waterfall's height from its top to the bedrock, or to the water surface (which often is several feet above the riverbed)? If the waterfall is composed of many descending ledges, does one count them all as one waterfall for purposes of height, or count the major drops as separate waterfalls?

Even when scientifically measured, height ultimately remains subjective. A 50-foot waterfall may look minuscule in a gorge whose walls are 200 feet high, but absolutely enormous in a ravine no deeper than 60 feet.

DEFACEMENT OF WATERFALLS

Anybody caught defacing waterfalls should be prosecuted to the fullest extent of the law. Too many rocks and trees already have initials carved into them by humans who gave into the impulse to leave their mark. Resist the urge to leave a message for posterity. If you find yourself tempted, just remember that all too soon your name will be permanently chiseled into a slab of stone. Why rush matters?

DEGREE OF DIFFICULTY

The following criteria were used to determine the degree of difficulty for the hikes in this book:

Easy—less than 1.0 mile one way, with mostly even terrain and minimal elevation change

Moderate—1.0 to 2.5 miles one way, with mixed terrain and some elevation change

Difficult—more than 2.5 miles one way, with significant elevation change and mixed terrain, possibly including some rock scrambling

A CONUNDRUM

The following puzzle is from Paul Sloane's fascinating book, *Lateral Thinking Puzzles* (Sterling Publishing Co., 1991). See if you can guess the answer.

"Although the people who come to see it think it moves forward, it actually moves backwards. It started about seven miles from where it is today and is moving now much slower than in the past. Previously, it traveled as much as five feet a year, but now it's traveling less than half that distance. Despite its slow speed, most of the people who have tried to ride along on it have perished in the attempt. What is it?

The answer? Niagara Falls.

CAUTION
Safety Tips

Outdoor recreational activities are by their very nature potentially hazardous and contain risk. All participants in such activities must assume the responsibility for their own actions and safety. No book can replace good judgment. The outdoors is forever changing. The author and the publisher cannot be held responsible for inaccuracies, errors or omissions, or for changes in the details of this publication, or for the consequences of any reliance on the information contained herein, or for the safety of people in the outdoors.

1. Dress appropriately—cotton clothing and sneakers are the number one cause of illness and injury leading to emergency evacuation. Wear proper sun protection—hat, sunglasses, sunscreen—appropriate to the season. Wear and use appropriate snow gear when the trails are snow-covered.

2. Be prepared: have a first aid kit, whistle, flashlight, matches, small tarp, extra high-energy food, and water (at least 24 ounces per person). Do not drink untreated water from streams.

3. Do not use or create shortcuts. These can be dangerous and encourage erosion.

4. Respect private property rights. Do not trespass. Get permission before entering private land.

5. Avoid rock climbing around waterfalls. Keep in mind that gorges containing waterfalls are composed of rocks that have been worn smooth over the centuries by running water and are slippery when wet or moss-covered.

6. Don't rely upon pre-existing ropes that others have set up for ascending or descending into a gorge. There is no way to know

how long that rope has been hanging from that tree or boulder, or what condition it's in. Even a rope that looks strong could be ready to give way at the next tug. Better to leave the rope alone than to discover that there's a problem after you are hanging over the rim of an 80-foot-high gorge.

7. Always keep a safe distance from the exposed edge of a precipitous gorge. Stand where there are trees and other objects to grab hold of should you begin to lose your footing.

8. Avoid taking young children or pets unless you are prepared to closely supervise them at all times, especially if you are hiking in along slippery rocks or approaching the top of a gorge.

9. Always maintain three points of contact while climbing up or down the sloping wall of a ravine.

10. Always make sure that someone knows your route and destination and expected time of arrival back home, especially when going out alone.

11. Do not walk or swim in the stream bed near the top of a waterfall. Remember that rocks when wet or mossy can be extremely slippery. Bear in mind, also, that the tops of some falls slope downward at a very gentle angle, drawing you ever closer to the edge where you may find yourself starting to slide and unable to stop. T-Lake Falls in the Adirondacks, and Kaaterskill Falls in the Catskills, for instance, have claimed the lives of a number of hikers who ventured out too near their tops for closer looks. Stay away from the top and enjoy the view from the side.

12. Leave the area immediately if you become accidentally immersed in water during the early spring, late fall, or winter. Recognize the possibility of quick-acting hypothermia, and get into the warmth of your car as soon as possible. To be extra safe, always carry a change of clothing in your car. Getting dry quickly is one sure way of warding off hypothermia.

13. Never dive headfirst into a water hole at the base of a waterfall. It is impossible to know with absolute certainty what may lie just below the surface. Too many people have ignored this commonsense rule and now travel in wheelchairs.

14. Never jump or dive from the top of the gorge or from high ledges into the water below. You may find yourself slipping and tumbling onto the rocks, instead of into the water.

15. Wear long sleeve shirts and long pants to ward off black fly and mosquito bites, and to reduce the risk of contracting Lyme disease through contact with an infected deer tick.

16. Heed signs and trail markers. Nature is always in flux. Routes described in this book may change or be altered in subtle but significant ways by the time you attempt to follow them.

17. Know where you are and where you are going at all times. Never go hiking without a map and compass. GPS units are highly recommended.

18. Take along a hiking stick or pole, especially if you plan to ford a stream. Hiking poles that compress into a small shaft for storage in backpacks are available in sporting goods stores.

Be prepared, be careful, have fun, and if you carry it in, carry it out!

FALLS ALONG ROUTE 30

Along Sacandaga River,
Foothills, Adirondack Mountains.

Route 30 follows the Sacandaga River.

The section of Rt. 30 between Northville and Tupper Lake passes by a series of pretty lakes and small towns. Between Northville and Speculator, Rt. 30 follows along a river valley system created by the Sacandaga River, a main tributary to the Hudson River. There are several waterfalls in the Northville area and near Wells, a small village between Northville and Speculator.

Several miles north of Wells, Rt. 8 takes you northeast, paralleling, for a time, the East Branch of the Sacandaga River. Several tributaries to the East Branch have produced a number of striking waterfalls along this segment of road.

Proceeding north again on Rt. 30 from the junction of Rts. 30 & 8, there are more waterfalls to visit as you continue along the west side of the Sacandaga River.

In Speculator, a side diversion on Rt. 8 takes you to two waterfalls, both of which are in the general area of Piseco Lake. From Speculator, Rt. 30 continues north, passing by one lake after another, including Indian Lake, Blue Mountain Lake, Long Lake, and Tupper Lake. There are several waterfalls to see along this part of Rt. 30, including Death Falls in Raquette Lake, Buttermilk Falls in Deerland, and Bog River Falls in Tupper Lake.

ROUTE 30

BEECHER CREEK FALLS

Location: Edinburg (Saratoga County)

Accessibility: Roadside: wheelchair accessible via a wide, 30-foot-long, descending path to covered bridge

Description: This 20-foot cascade is formed on Beecher Creek, a medium-sized stream that rises from Old Pond and Greenfield Lake, and flows into the Great Sacandaga Lake at Beecher Hollow.

The falls consist of a series of ledges, almost stair-like in appearance, located in Beechers Hollow.

History: Beecher Creek and the falls are named after Eli Beecher (1777-1865), an early settler who dammed up the creek and built a sawmill a short distance downstream from the falls.

In the past Beecher Creek had been heavily industrialized. At one time, nine mills and factories were operating along the creek from Tenantville (north of the falls) down to Beecher Hollow, including a machine shop, grist & mill shop, blacksmith shop, factory for making coffins, cabinets and furniture, carriage shop, tannery, and lumber & broom handle shop.

The picturesque covered bridge located just downstream from the falls is a 29-foot-long queen post truss bridge, constructed in 1879 by Arad Copeland so that his cows could cross the creek and graze on the grasses further down in the valley. Since 1930 such forages have become impossible. The Great Sacandaga Lake now rests where the spacious valley once existed.

Directions: From Amsterdam (junction of Rts. 5 & 30) take Rt. 30 north to Vail Mills, then proceed east into Broadalbin. From Broadalbin (which is located on the southeast corner of the Great Sacandaga Lake) go north on North Street, which quickly turns into County Rt. 110. Continue north on Rt. 110, which eventually becomes County Rt. 7—all the time paralleling the lake, which will remain on your left. When you come to the tiny hamlet of Batchellerville, cross over the Batchellerville Bridge and proceed west up a steep hill. At the top of the hill, you will be in the tiny hamlet of Edinburg. Turn right onto Rt. 4 at the main intersection, and follow the road downhill (going northeast) for about 0.5 miles. Pull off to your right just before you get to the covered bridge. Follow a short walkway leading down to the stream and across the covered bridge for views of the fall.

Driving across the Batchellerville Bridge—over .6 mile long—is part of the adventure to Beecher Creek Falls.

WEST STONY CREEK FALLS

Location: Near Northville (Hamilton County)

Accessibility: 1.5-mile hike (one way) over fairly easy terrain, mostly following an old dirt road

Difficulty Level: Moderate

Description: This waterfall is formed on the North Branch of West Stony Creek, a medium-sized tributary that rises in the hills west of Upper Benson and ultimately flows into the Sacandaga River several miles north of Northville.

Although only four feet in height, the fall is very pretty and located just downstream from a rustic, log footbridge that spans the creek.

History: The fall is located along the famous Northville-Placid Trail, which was established in 1922 by the Adirondack Mountain Club (ADK) and is now maintained by the NYS Department of Environmental Conservation.

According to the *Guide to Adirondack Trails: Northville-Placid Trail*, a previous footbridge spanned the North Branch upstream from the falls, but was damaged in 1978 and had to be removed.

Directions: From Northville take Rt. 30 northwest for 3.2 miles. Immediately after crossing over West Stony Creek, turn left onto County Rt. 6 (there are signs that point the way to Benson and the

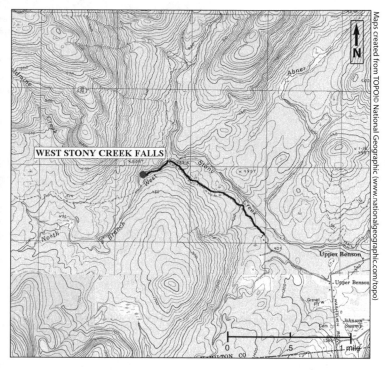

Northville-Placid Trail) and drive west, going slowly uphill. After driving for 5.2 miles along Rt. 6, you will pass the right-hand turn for the Lapland Lake Ski Touring Center. Continue straight. At 5.8 miles, after crossing over an old iron bridge, the road immediately forks. Go right, following the signs for the Northville-Placid Trail, and continue northwest for 0.6 mile. Turn left onto a dirt road (listed as Godfrey Road on the *NYS Atlas & Gazetteer*) where a sign indicates the way to Rock Lake and Star Lake, and continue for another 0.5 mile. Park in a designated area on the right.

Proceed on foot, following the dirt road (occasionally marked by blue-blazed markers) as it passes by the rustic headquarters of the United Rod and Gun Club. You will see posted signs on both sides of the road. Stay on the road, which provides an easement through this privately-owned tract of land. Continue walking for 1.2 miles going northwest and gradually gaining elevation, only to lose some of it as you descend to a point where the dirt road ends, which will be at the North Branch of West Stony Creek. Follow a blue-blazed tote road northwest for 0.3 mile as it parallels the North Branch. You will soon come to the falls, which are just downstream from a massive, log footbridge that spans the creek.

FALLS ALONG RIVER ROAD

Location: North of Northville (Hamilton County)

Accessibility: Roadside

Description: This small cascade is formed on an unnamed stream that rises on the east shoulder of Cathead Mountain and flows into the Sacandaga River a short distance downstream from the falls. The cascade, which consists of a series of drops, is over 40 feet in height, but generally not very impressive because of the meager amount of water carried by the tiny creek.

If you are interested in seeing the waterfall at its best, visit in early spring when the creek is overflowing from snow melt.

Directions: From Northville take Rt. 30 north for 3.2 miles. Turn left onto County Rt. 6 (which leads to Benson, and the trailhead to Cathead Mountain) and then immediately turn right onto River Road. River Road, as implied by its name, follows the west bank of the Sacandaga River. Drive north for roughly 1.5 miles. The falls will be visible on your left.

FALLS ON GROFF CREEK

Location: North of Northville (Hamilton County)

Accessibility: 1.8-mile hike (one way) over an old road and then an ascending path

Difficulty Level: Difficult: requires a scramble down a steep, 100-foot slope to see the falls close up

Description: There are two medium-sized waterfalls and one small waterfall formed on Groff Creek, a small stream that rises in the hills between Wallace Mountain and Southerland Mountain and flows east around the shoulder of Groff Mountain into the Sacandaga River at a point mid-way between Hope and Pumpkin Hollow.

The first waterfall is approximately 30 feet in height, consisting of a gently inclined, long slide into a basin pool, followed by a 5-foot drop. The basin, which is fairly large, is enclosed on both sides by curved walls.

The second waterfall consists of a large, 15-foot-high block of rock over which the stream plunges into a pool below.

The third fall—the most readily accessible—is a 10-foot-high cascade.

Directions: From Northville take Rt. 30 north for 3.2 miles. Turn left onto County Rt. 6 and then immediately right onto River Road. Drive north for 4.6 miles, paralleling the Sacandaga River the entire way. When you reach the end of the traversable road, park and continue north on foot, going steadily downhill.

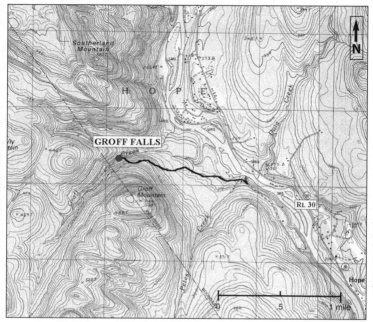

Within 0.5 mile the dirt road leads to Peters Creek, where a wooden bridge takes you over the stream just above the creek's confluence with the Sacandaga River. An imposing cement block building will be visible on your left. Continue following the road as it proceeds uphill. After 0.4 mile, the road veers to the right at a fork and quickly becomes a wide path. Groff Creek now comes into view on your right, but then disappears, only to reappear later when the trail begins ascending the shoulder of a steep hill.

The first fall is reached in roughly 0.7 mile from the fork. It is difficult to see from the trail, but it is quite audible. A 100-foot descent down the sloping bank will take you to the top of the fall. The second fall is approximately 0.2 mile further upstream and is visible from the trail. It is possible to descend the steep slope for a closer look. The third fall is 0.1 mile upstream and also visible from the trail. Gaining a closer look at this cascade is not as difficult as for the first two falls, but still involves negotiating a steep bank leading down to the stream.

TENANT CREEK FALLS

Location: Hope Falls (Hamilton County)

Accessibility: 0.5-mile hike (one way) along uneven terrain, with little elevation gain

Difficulty Level: Easy to Moderate

Description: Tenant Creek Falls is a pretty cascade formed on Tenant Creek, a medium-sized stream that rises from Tenant Lake and flows into East Stony Creek about a half-mile below the falls. The falls are formed at a point where the creek makes a sharp turn, changing direction from north to northwest. Tenant Creek Falls is over 40 feet high and consists of steeply layered slabs of rock.

A wonderful swimming hole can be found at the base of the falls and can be easily accessed from the west bank, which is nearly level with the stream.

The falls consist of a number of small drops and plunges. This author once saw a dog swept over the top of the falls. It rode the cascade down on all four legs, as though on a slide, plunging the last seven or eight feet over the lip of the final drop and into the pool at the waterfall's base. Fortunately, the dog survived—although momentarily stunned.

For the adventurous hiker with time and energy to spare, there are two more waterfalls upstream, slightly over 1.5 miles from the main falls. The first upstream waterfall is a small cascade, while the second is a 20-foot cascade into a pool of water.

№ 621. Pleasure Drive in the Mountains (Adirondacks) on the Road to Hope, N. Y.

The town of Hope is gone, but Tenant Creek Falls remains.

History: Tenant Creek Falls is also called Hope Falls because of its close proximity to the once-thriving village of Hope Falls. The village, which once consisted of a number of tanneries, mills, and houses, turned into a ghost town in the early 1900s and has vanished almost completely now.

Directions: From Amsterdam proceed north on Rt. 30 to Northville. Cross over the Northville Bridge into the village of Northville, driving east on Bridge Street. Turn left onto Main Street, drive north for 0.2 mile, and then turn left onto Reed Street just before heading up a steep hill. Follow Reed Street west, and then north as it turns into Old State Highway and parallels the Great Sacandaga Lake (on your left). After 3 miles you will reach a right-hand turn where a sign indicates the way to Hope Falls. Drive northeast for almost 3 miles (with East Stony Creek on your left). Take your third left (ignoring the first two turns, which take you into Hope Falls) and continue north. East Stony Creek will come back quickly on your left again. When the macadam ends, proceed along a hard-packed dirt road for another 1.5 miles until you reach the end of the road (where a private lane leads to the old Brownell

Camp). From where you turned off of Old State Highway, the distance to the trailhead parking is about 7.4 miles.

From the parking area follow the trail north along East Stony Creek for less than 0.1 mile. You will see a very attractive footbridge spanning Tenant Creek. Just before the bridge is a well-worn trail that goes off to the right along the south bank. Follow this path east for 0.5 mile and you will arrive at the falls.

To see the upper two falls, which are less than 2 miles away from the parking area, follow a less well-worn trail paralleling the creek along the south bank as you proceed upstream.

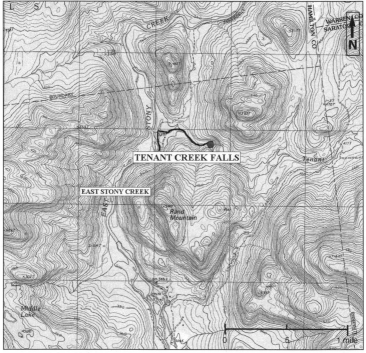

Maps created from TOPO!© National Geographic (www.nationalgeographic.com/topo)

FALLS ON THE WEST BRANCH OF THE SACANDAGA RIVER

Location: Near Whitehouse (Hamilton County)

Accessibility: 2.5-mile hike (one way) over uneven terrain; hike should be undertaken in mid-summer when water level is low

Difficulty Level: Moderate

Description: There are two relatively small, but striking waterfalls formed on the middle section of the West Branch of the Sacandaga River, a fairly large stream that rises from several sources (including Meco Lake, Rock Lake, White Lake, and Silver Lake) in a remote area of the southern Adirondacks and joins with the Sacandaga River several miles south of Wells virtually across from the Sacandaga Campgrounds.

The first waterfall is located about 0.25 mile upstream from the east end of the West Branch Gorge, a deep and rugged gully with walls that loom 400 feet high in places, and with a relief of over 240 feet from its beginning to its end. The waterfall is formed at a point where the gorge is narrow. Huge boulders the size of small buildings and automobiles are strewn all about the base and sides of the waterfall, making it a wonderful place to explore interesting nooks and crannies. There are even several tiny, talus caves formed in the jumble of rocks, and one huge, table-like rock shelter that is impossible to miss on the climb up along the north bank to the top of the falls. Rivulets of water cascade down between the heaps of rocks and boulders.

The falls are no more than 10-12 feet high, but seem to loom much larger because of the spectacular, encasing piles of rocks. At the top of the falls along the north bank can be found a huge fissure where a house-sized boulder has split apart, forming a passageway 20 feet in length. Even on the hottest summer day, the temperature at the back of this fissure remains delightfully cool.

Remnants abound of the West Branch's fury in early spring. On my last hike through the gorge, the twisted and battered remains of a canoe were observed a short distance downstream from the falls. One can only hope that the paddlers as well were not swept over the falls and through the rocky gorge! In some narrow sections of the gorge, high-water marks are 20 feet above the mid-summer level of the stream bed, further evidence that this is not a river to trifle with during its torrential season.

Hiking through the gorge should only be attempted from mid-summer to late fall, when there is a reduced flow of water. In the spring the water sweeps through the gorge with tremendous force.

One cannot see the second falls from the top of the first waterfall because of the curvature of the gorge, even though the two are separated by a distance of only several hundred yards. The second falls is a pretty, 6 to 8-foot cascade that flows through a narrow stricture in the gorge upstream from the first falls. When seen from afar, the cascade looks like a continuous curtain of falling water.

The second falls contains its fair share of large boulders and rocks as well, but there is nothing in size to rival the magnitude of the debris at the first falls.

As you stand near the base of the falls, glance up to the northeast, downstream and upwards towards your left, in order to glimpse sections of the high cliffs overlooking the gorge.

Continue further west through the gorge and you will eventually come upon two more small falls, including one just below where Piseco Lake Outlet joins the West Branch.

Directions: Take Rt. 30 north from Northville to Wells. As you enter Wells, turn left onto Algonquin Road (passing by a dam at the outlet to Lake Algonquin) and then drive southwest for 0.7 mile. Turn left onto West River Road and continue west for a little over 8 miles. (Note: after you have driven several miles, the road will

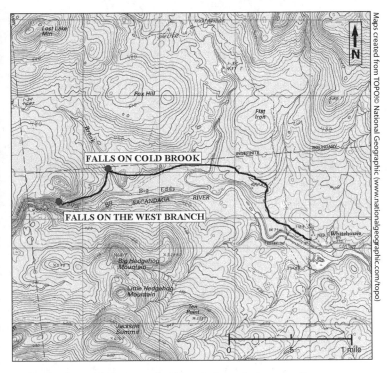

change from blacktop to hard-packed earth, but it remains quite passable.) Roughly 8.3 miles from Lake Algonquin, the road ends as you drive into a huge parking area. This is the site of the former Whitehouse Lodge and is frequented by hunters. From here, you will continue on foot.

A path leads northwest from the parking lot. Within a moment or two, you will pass by a trail on your left that leads to Canary Pond and the Mud Lake lean-to. Continue on the main trail. At approximately 0.5-0.6 mile, a path goes off to your left. Follow this secondary trail as it leads uphill. Within 0.1 mile you will reach another path, an old, abandoned road that has become trail-like over time. Turn left onto this path and continue west for roughly 0.5 mile. This trail will lead you to Hamilton Lake Stream, a difficult stream to ford during high waters, which is why this hike should be taken only in mid-summer when crossing is easy. A narrow suspension bridge used to cross the stream, but unfortunately is no longer present.

Pick up the trail on the opposite side of Hamilton Lake Stream and hike west through the woods for another 0.1 mile. You will come out onto the West Branch of the Sacandaga River just downstream from an area of rapids known as Big Eddy. From this point the rest of the hike is fairly straightforward. Follow the West Branch upstream, going west along its north bank. There is a small path that winds along the side of the north bank that can be followed for most of the distance, making the route traversable even during high waters. It is also possible to walk along the rocks on several sections of the stream bed as long as you are not undertaking the hike in early spring.

As you hike along the West Branch, at about 0.6 mile upstream from Big Eddy, you will pass by a pretty waterfall on Cold Brook (see following chapter) at its confluence with the West Branch.

After another 0.6 mile you will reach the first falls. For experienced hikers wishing to see the second falls, it is possible to climb up and over the large boulders to get to the top of the falls.

From the top of the falls, just up from where the stream plunges over, it is then possible to make your way around a large wall of rock on the north bank (if the water level is low) and stroll effortlessly up to the second falls, which is only several hundred yards away. If the river is too deep or fierce at the first fall's top, you will find it necessary to hike around a rocky mound on the north side of the falls and then descend to the floor of the gorge between the two falls. From the base of the second falls, a fairly easy path takes you right up the north bank to the top of the waterfall.

The other option for viewing the second falls is to cross over to the south bank, climb up to the top of the ravine, and look down from afar, but be warned that the view will be less intimate.

FALLS ON COLD BROOK

Location: Hamilton County (Note: This waterfall can be seen on the way to the Falls on the West Branch of the Sacandaga River)

Accessibility: 2.0-mile hike (one way) over uneven terrain, with rock hop across stream

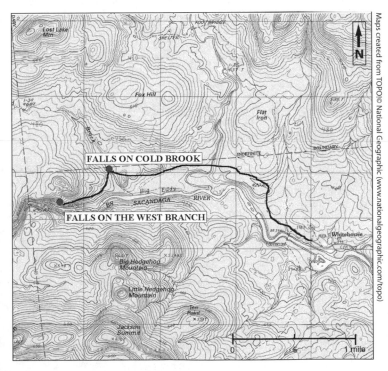

Maps created from TOPO!© National Geographic (www.nationalgeographic.com/topo)

Difficulty Level: Moderate

Description: This pretty waterfall chute is formed on Cold Brook, a small stream that rises north of Mud Lake Mountain, is fed by several tributaries including one from Lost Lake, and flows into the West Branch of the Sacandaga River between the West Branch Gorge and Big Eddy.

The waterfall is formed at the stream's confluence with the West Branch, and consists of two distinct sections. The first is a tiny waterfall produced where the stream flows around a large boulder and falls 4 to 5 feet. The second is a long chute totaling 20 feet in height where the stream tumbles through a fairly steep ravine.

Directions: Follow the directions given for the Falls on the West Branch to reach the West Branch of the Sacandaga River. Then follow the trail west along the north bank for approximately 0.6 mile. As you approach Cold Brook, you will hear the high-spirited sound of the waterfall even before you see it.

AUGER FALLS

Location: North of Wells (Hamilton County)

Accessibility: 0.3-mile hike (one way) over uneven terrain

Difficulty Level: Easy

Description: Auger Falls is formed on the Sacandaga River, a moderately large stream that rises from Lake Pleasant and flows into the Hudson River at Hadley & Lake Luzerne.

Auger Falls consists of a series of drops and plunges with a total relief of roughly 100 feet, contained in a very narrow, rocky gorge. According to the ADK's *Guide to Adirondack Trails: Central Region*, "three distinct cataracts are seen." The main waterfall is approximately 40 feet high with a rocky outcrop at the top that cleaves the stream into two cascades.

Undoubtedly the name Auger Falls originated when an early visitor noted that the ravine had been bored out as though by an enormous auger. Scouring of the river bed continues, although on a much smaller scale. When the water level is down, numerous potholes can be seen in the stream bed and along the side of the ravine.

The name Auger is not unique to these falls; there is also Auger Hole Falls on the St. Regis River near Tupper Lake, and Screw Auger Falls in Grafton Notch, Maine.

The valley enclosing Auger Falls—from Austin Falls to the Rt. 8 bridge crossing over the Sacandaga River—is described by Walter F. Burmeister in *The Hudson Valley and its Tributaries*, as a "wooded valley, enclosed by 800 foot slopes beyond the right shore, and 1100 foot slopes above the left shore." As you drive up from Wells on Rt. 30, you will see this immense canyon to your right shortly after passing the junction with Rt. 8.

On the west bank of the gorge is an intriguing fissure cave, caused by a section of rock fracturing and being displaced from the main body. The slippage has created an enterable fissure, some 2 feet wide and 10-15 feet deep. Ice and snow linger at the bottom of the passageway until mid-summer.

Directions: From Wells drive north on Rt. 30 to the junction of Rts. 30 & 8. Continue north on Rt. 30 for 1.7 miles, then turn right into a dirt parking area. Park in the upper section of the lot and walk along a four-wheel-drive road leading south and paralleling Rt. 30 for 0.1 mile. (Note: You can drive this easily in a four-wheel-drive vehicle.)

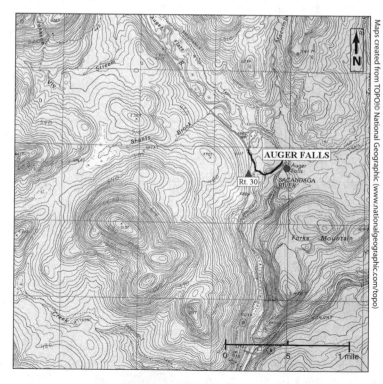

When you reach the end of the four-wheel-drive road, turn left and follow the trail into the woods. You will know that you are on the right trail when you arrive at the trailhead register. Sign in and continue east along the path, following the yellow-blazed markers on the trees. The hike in is no more than ten minutes long. Well before you reach the gorge, you will begin to hear the mighty roar of Auger Falls.

The trail ultimately leads to the mouth of the gorge where the river rounds a sharp bend and then begins its plunge through the chasm. There is a wonderful overlook of the falls just a short distance downstream from this point.

AUSTIN FALLS

Location: South of Speculator (Hamilton County)

Accessibility: Near roadside; short, 40-foot scramble down river bank

Difficulty Level: Easy

Description: Austin Falls is a long, waterslide flume that is formed on the Sacandaga River, a sizable stream that rises from Lake Pleasant and flows into the Hudson River at Hadley & Lake Luzerne. The falls are located nearly midway between Auger Falls to the south and Christine Falls to the north.

The waters are exceedingly calm and placid above the falls, but as the waterfall approaches, the river bed becomes very narrow. The Sacandaga River becomes compressed, accelerated, and incredibly agitated. Within 300 yards, a 40-foot drop advances the raging waters on a roller coaster ride. According to the ADK *Guide to Adirondack Trails: Central Region*, "The charm of this section of river is the potpourri of geological ocean-bottom evidence in the rock, pot holes, rock channels, polished rock, and glacial striae (grooved bedrock) found as one walks beside the fast-flowing water upstream from the falls."

A large boulder near the base of the falls catapults the water rushing over it 3 feet or more into the air, creating a huge wave.

Directions: From Wells drive north on Rt. 30 to the junction of Rts. 30 & 8. Continue north on Rt. 30 for over 6.5 miles. Turn right onto a paved, secondary road (Old Rt. 30) and drive southeast for 2.7 miles. Bear in mind that this is a seasonal road and is not maintained from December 1 to April 1. Drive cautiously, for the road has buckled. Near the end of the drive, you will be paralleling the Sacandaga River. Pull over to the side of the road at 2.7 miles. There are several paths that lead down to the stream and falls, which are only 50 feet away.

If you inadvertently drive by Austin Falls, you will end up at the southern end of Old Rt. 30, which is marked by an abandoned bridge crossing the Sacandaga River and leading back to Rt. 30. Turn around and drive north for 0.8 mile. Austin Falls will now be on your left.

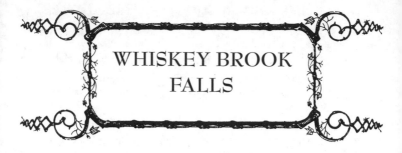

WHISKEY BROOK FALLS

Location: Near Speculator (Hamilton County)

Accessibility: Near roadside; less than 0.05 mile from road, over uneven terrain

Difficulty Level: Easy

Description: This tiny waterfall is formed on Hatchery Brook, a small creek that rises on the southwest shoulder of East Mountain and flows into the north end of Sacandaga Lake (not to be confused with the Great Sacandaga Lake, which is further south). Whiskey Brook, from which the fall is named, is a small tributary of Hatchery Brook.

The waterfall is 5 to 6 feet in height and encased by huge boulders that litter the stream bed as well.

Directions: From Northville drive north on Rt. 30 until you reach the village of Speculator. Continue north on Rt. 30 for 2.2 miles from the junction of Rts. 30 & 8. As you approach the 2.2-mile mark, look very carefully to your right to glimpse the small stream, which is channeled under Rt. 30 through a drainpipe.

Park off on the right and follow the south bank of the small creek upstream for approximately 50 feet until you reach the fall.

DUG MOUNTAIN BROOK FALLS

Location: Indian Lake (Hamilton County)

Accessibility: 7.0-mile+ canoe paddle (one way), followed by a short hike

Difficulty Level: Difficult

Description: Dug Mountain Brook Falls are formed on Dug Mountain Brook, a small stream that rises in the hills southeast of

Prospectors found more than gold in the foothills above Indian Lake when they started up Dug Mountain Brook.

Indian Lake and flows into the Jessup River at Jessup Bay (where Indian Lake and the Jessup River merge).

There is a small waterfall at the confluence of Dug Mountain Brook and the Jessup River. The main waterfall is further upstream and consists of a 40-foot cascade.

Directions: To get to Indian Lake, go north on Rt. 30 from Speculator. Eventually you will pass the entrance to the Lewey Lake Campgrounds on your left. Immediately after, pull into the entrance to the Indian Lake Campgrounds on your right just before you cross over a stream connecting Indian Lake with Lewey Lake.

From the state campground at the southern end of Indian Lake, canoe northeast across the lake for over 2 miles. When you get to Long Island, veer to the east and then paddle southwest into a narrow passageway that forms the river-like portion of Indian Lake.

When you reach the end of Indian Lake at Jessup Bay—past the point where the lake is at its narrowest—you will see Dug Mountain Brook on your left along the bay's eastern shore. Pull up your canoe at this point.

To reach the upper, main waterfall, follow a trail along the north bank of Dug Mountain Brook and hike east for 0.4 mile. You will arrive at the base of the 40-foot-high cataract.

If you enjoy camping in semi-wilderness, you can combine this waterfall trek with an overnight stay at one of the state campsites along Indian Lake (just be sure to call ahead to reserve a site).

An alternate, shorter paddle to the falls is available from where Rt. 30 crosses the Jessup River, slightly over a mile south of Mason Lake (6 miles south of Indian Lake). From there proceed northeast along the stream until you reach Dug Mountain Brook on your right. Note that this part of the Jessup River is prone to blowdown and may require negotiating around obstacles along the way.

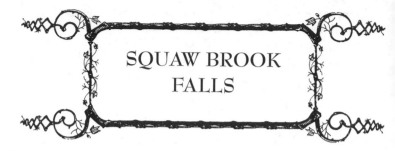

SQUAW BROOK
FALLS

Location: Indian Lake (Hamilton County)

Accessibility: Roadside

Description: This tiny waterfall situated in a small, rocky gorge, is formed on Squaw Brook, a small stream that rises northwest of Snowy Mountain and flows into Indian Lake north of Sabael. Though not especially scenic nor easy to glimpse in its entirety, the fall has an interesting history.

Squaw Brook and Bridge, Indian Lake, Adirondacks, N.Y.

Squaw Brook may be obscure, but it has centuries of history.

History: The falls are named after Margaret, wife (or "squaw") of Sabael Benedict—a Penobscot Indian and the first settler at Indian Lake (around the time of the American Revolutionary War). Margaret was buried at the mouth of Squaw Brook. Indian Lake was named after Sabael. Indian Lake was originally a series of three smaller lakes until the northern end was dammed, creating one large area of water. Long ago, Snowy Mountain, which looms above Indian Lake, was known as Squaw Bonnet Mountain in further tribute to Benedict's wife. The name was changed to Snowy Mountain because landslides have exposed areas of white rock.

Directions from the north: From Indian Lake Village take Rt. 30 south for 3.4 miles. You will cross over a small bridge. The falls and gorge are directly below on the east side. Stay on the road and bridge to view the falls and gorge. Don't trespass on private lands.

Directions from the south: At the south end of Indian Lake, you will cross over a stream connecting Lewey Lake and Indian Lake. Drive northeast for 8 miles. The falls are directly below a small bridge.

DEATH FALLS

Location: Raquette Lake (Hamilton County)

Accessibility 0.2-mile walk (one way) over fairly level terrain

Difficulty Level: Easy

Description: Death Falls is a large cascade over 70 feet high formed on a tiny tributary to Death Brook, a small stream that rises in the hills above Rt. 28 and flows into Raquette Lake near Golden Beach. Despite its low volume of water, this fall is appealing because it cascades over a wide cliff face.

Death Brook is one of several small tributaries to Raquette Lake.

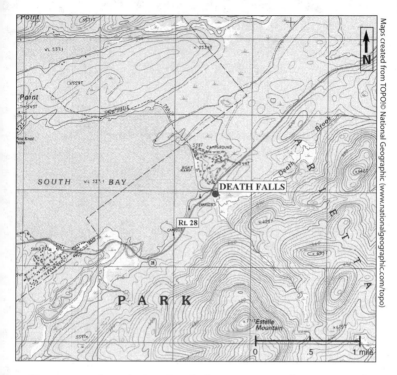

Maps created from TOPO!© National Geographic (www.nationalgeographic.com/topo)

Directions: From the Hamlet of Blue Mountain Lake (junction of Rts. 28 & 30), drive southwest on Rt. 28 for 9.4 miles. Look to your left for a yellow gate and a yellow sign stating: "Stop. Barrier Ahead." Turn around and park in the pull-off by the gate.

From the gate, follow an old, grassy road southwest for 0.1 mile. You will come out into a large, open, grassy area. Continue southeast, entering woods again, and follow the road as it narrows, becoming more path-like. Soon you will pass a small, open area on your right where a large number of scattered limestone blocks can be seen—remnants of a former structure. Just past this point you will see to your left a path going off from the main trail. Take that path, because it bypasses a swampy area along the main trail. The bypass trail quickly reconnects with the main trail past the swamp, which then leads up to the base of the fall.

BUTTERMILK
FALLS

Location: Near Deerland (Hamilton County)

Accessibility: Short walk, less than 0.05 mile (one way) over fairly level ground

Difficulty Level: Easy

Description: Buttermilk Falls is formed on the Raquette River, a medium-sized stream that rises from Raquette Lake and ultimately flows into the St. Lawrence River. The cascade drops a total of 40 feet over a series of terraces.

Buttermilk Falls is one of the Adirondacks' most frequently visited waterfalls.

Seneca Ray Stoddard, the famous nineteenth-century writer, photographer, and popularizer of the Adirondacks, summed it up very well in *The Adirondacks Illustrated*: "Here the water dashes and foams down the rock, making a descent of about twenty feet, and the name, though not very poetical, was probably suggested by the churning that it gets in reaching the bottom." Buttermilk Falls, of course, is about as generic a name for a waterfall as one is likely to encounter—the equivalent of "Bald Mountain" for a mountain peak with exposed rock. There are numerous Buttermilk Falls in New York State, including well known ones at Leeds (in the Catskills), LeRoy (near Rochester), and Buttermilk Falls State Park in Ithaca.

There are excellent views of the falls from along the east bank, where one can stand at practically the same level as the stream.

Near the base of the falls can be seen an energetic chute, where waters smash into a huge boulder before moving off into calm, sluggish waters.

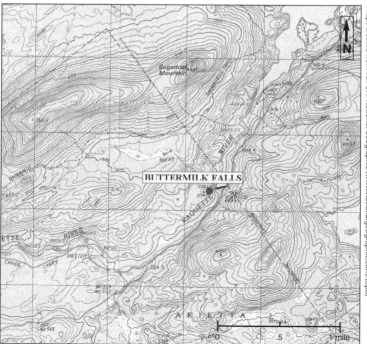

Maps created from TOPO!© National Geographic (www.nationalgeographic.com/topo)

There are many other falls on the Raquette River, including Raquette Falls near Raquette Lake, and Hedgehog Rapids, Moosehead Rapids, Moody Falls, Jamestown Falls, Halls Rapids, Stark Falls, Blake Falls, Little Falls, Leonard Falls, Rankin Falls, and Five Falls (the latter five have been flooded by hydro-electric dams), all between Piercefield and South Colton.

History: Buttermilk Falls is a well known, advertised tourist attraction, and has been for many years.

Early French explorers named Raquette Lake (the headwaters of the Raquette River) after the French word for "snowshoe." According to legend, loyalist Sir John Johnson abandoned a pile of snowshoes in 1776 as he fled to Canada during the Revolutionary War.

Except for the Hudson River, the Raquette, at 153 miles, is the longest river in New York State. Native American Indians called the river *Ta-na-wa-deh*, meaning "swift water." Long Lake was called *In-ca-pah-co*. To early settlers Long Lake was known as Lindenmere because of the linden trees covering the nearby hillsides.

Directions: From Blue Mountain Lake (junction of Rts. 30, 28, & 28N) drive north on Rt. 30/28N until you reach Deerland, which is several miles southwest of the village of Long Lake. Turn left onto North Point Road (where a sign indicates the way to Buttermilk Falls) and drive southwest for 2.1 miles. You will see an elongated pull-off on your right and a sign for Buttermilk Falls.

Follow a short trail less than 0.05 mile to the falls.

BOG RIVER FALLS

Location: Tupper Lake (Franklin County)

Accessibility: Roadside view of upper falls; 50-foot scramble to stream bed to see lower falls

Difficulty Level: Easy

Description: Bog River Falls is formed on the Bog River at the inlet to Tupper Lake. The Bog River is a medium-sized stream that flows out of Lows Lake, with significant tributaries from Bear Brook and the outflows from Round Lake and Little Tupper Lake.

The falls are two-tiered and would be fairly nondescript were it not for the volume of water carried by the stream and the broadness of the upper falls. The upper cascade is broken into smaller sections by two small, island-like areas at the top. The falls are rounded, fairly smooth, and only 6 to 8 feet high. The lower cascade is narrower and rockier, and the water races over the bedrock more energetically. The stone bridge spans this cascade, allowing a view of only the upper cascade from the bridge.

The view of the falls is enhanced at times by the presence of trout fishers standing in the shallow waters by their base.

According to *Adirondack Canoe Waters: North Flow*, the falls total 30 feet in relief.

Reference to the falls can be found in *Exploring the Adirondack Mountains 100 Years Ago*, edited by Stuart D. Ludlum: "At its head the wild and little-explored Bog River flows into the lake over a romantic cascade, which forms one of the great attractions of the

Adirondacks, being a famous place for trout, and having near by one of the most popular taverns of the wilderness, established a few years ago, and kept by Mr. Graves, who, in 1872, while hunting was accidentally killed by his son, being shot by him while aiming at a deer, with which his father was struggling in the water."

History: In "Mystery at Bog River Falls" by Mary MacKenzie, an article in the summer 1973 issue of *Adirondack Life*, the author writes that a lumberman named Franklin Jenkins established a "chopping and saw mill at Bog River Falls."

The "mystery of Bog River Falls" centers around a huge, 1000-year-old porcelain vase that allegedly was found sometime after 1855 in the tangled roots of a downed tree. The vase was broken into six pieces in order that it could be divided equally between the six finders, but none of the pieces has survived ... or so the story goes.

Directions: Take Rt. 30 north to the Village of Long Lake. Cross over the bridge spanning a narrow section of the lake, and continue north on Rt. 30 for 12.6 miles. Just before reaching the edge of Tupper Lake, turn left onto Rt. 421 and drive northwest for 0.7 mile. After crossing over an old stone bridge, immediately pull into

Bog River Falls is a fisherman's paradise.

the parking area on your left. A pathway leads down to the base of the upper falls.

To get a good look at the lower falls, walk across the bridge to its east end and follow a small footpath down the embankment to the edge of Long Lake. A little peninsula of rock partially extends in front of the falls, allowing for excellent views of the cascades and stone bridge.

ROUTE 8 EAST

EAST JIMMY CREEK FALLS

Location: North of Wells (Hamilton County)

Accessibility: Short hike, less than 0.1 mile (one way) over uneven terrain

Difficulty Level: Easy

Description: These pretty falls are formed on (East) Jimmy Creek, a small stream that rises near Smith Mountain and joins with the East Branch of the Sacandaga River several miles north of Wells.

These falls should not be confused with the cascade on (West) Jimmy Creek near Blackbridge. Although the streams share the same name and are located in the vicinity of Wells, they are not connected to one another nor all that close in proximity, being separated by a good 7 miles.

There are two falls on (East) Jimmy Creek. The main waterfall is 8 to 10 feet in height and is formed in a stream bed filled with jumbles of green, mossy boulders. There is a small swimming hole at its base. This is a gem of a waterfall, especially considering how close it is to a main road. A series of small cascades and rapids can be seen above the fall.

The second fall is located at the beginning of the hike and is fairly undistinguished. It consists of a chute waterfall 4 feet in height but very elongated, formed where the bedding is slightly tilted, thus creating a funnel for the stream to come tumbling through.

According to a large-scale topo map, "The Adirondacks: Central Mountains," another waterfall is formed further up East

Jimmy Creek between Oak Hill and an unidentified hill of roughly 1900 feet in height. This fall is approximately two and a half miles from East Jimmy Creek's confluence with the East Branch of the Sacandaga River.

Directions: From Wells go north on Rt. 30 for roughly 3.5 miles until you come to the junction of Rts. 30 & 8. Turn right onto Rt. 8, cross over the East Branch of the Sacandaga River, and drive northeast for 1.2 miles. You will reach a point where pull-offs are visible on both sides of the road next to a small stream that is funneled under the road through a large drainpipe. Park to the right and follow a path along the south bank paralleling Jimmy Creek. The hike up to the main falls is less than 0.1 mile.

GRIFFIN FALLS

Location: North of Wells (Hamilton County)

Accessibility: Short hike, less than 0.1 mile (one way) over uneven terrain

Difficulty Level: Easy to Moderate

Description: Griffin Falls is formed on the East Branch of the Sacandaga River not too far upstream from its confluence with the main body of the Sacandaga River. The falls are located in a rocky gorge whose bedding is tilted to roughly a 45-degree angle. The falls consist of several drops over angular blocks of rock in an area where the stream drops 30 feet in 100 yards. The main fall is an 8-foot cascade. Although the waterfalls and rapids are pretty, it is the gorge itself that is the centerpiece.

History: You would never know it now, but a town named Griffin, consisting of over 250 buildings including two stores, two hotels, a telegraph office, and a saloon, once existed along the west bank of the East Branch of the Sacandaga River just across from the bridge as you go upstream. Griffin was settled in 1835 and was originally called Moon Mills. It was renamed Griffin in honor of Stephen Griffin, Jr., who ran a local tannery.

The old iron bridge that so prominently spans the river was constructed in 1903. It provides an excellent view downstream into the small gorge and the top of Griffin Falls. Major repairs on the bridge were undertaken in 2003.

Directions: From Wells proceed north on Rt. 30 for approximately 3.5 miles. Turn right onto Rt. 8 at the junction of Rts. 30 & 8 and drive northeast for roughly 2.5 miles. Look for a trail sign on your right that states: "Trail to Rt. 8 at George Brook. Cod Pond, Willis Lake." At this point you will see a dirt road going off on the opposite side of the road. Turn left and follow this seasonal road downhill (north) for 0.2 mile. As soon as you cross over the East Branch of the Sacandaga River, park off to the side of the road.

Follow the tiny footpath paralleling the west side of the river, going downstream. In less than 0.1 mile you will descend to the stream bed by the falls, where some scrambling over slabs of rock is required to get a good view.

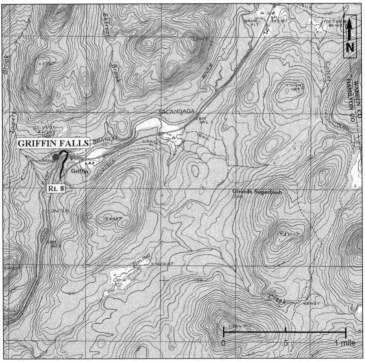

FALLS ON OREGON TRAIL

Location: Between Wells and Bakers Mills (Warren County)

Accessibility: Fairly undemanding hike, less than 1.0 mile (one way) with small change in elevation and some marshy areas

Difficulty Level: Easy to Moderate

Description: This small, chute cascade is formed at the marshy outlet to Cod Pond on a continuation of Stewarts Creek, a medium-sized stream that rises to the northeast from multiple tributaries in the mountainous Wilcox Lake Wild Forest area.

The cascade is formed in a tiny gorge where the bedding is slab-like and slightly tilted. A well-constructed bridge for hikers and snowmobilers spans the stream at the top of the gorge. This is a very picturesque area, containing the falls, a tiny gorge, a wooden bridge, and a huge marshland extending to the east.

Directions: From Wells continue north on Rt. 30 for around 3.5 miles. At the junction of Rts. 30 & 8, turn right onto Rt. 8 and drive northeast for 8.6 miles. You will see a pull-off on your right, and a state marker indicating Cod Pond.

From the trailhead proceed east. After 0.2 mile you will cross over what was once a trail intersection, but which now has been reduced (because of blowdown) to the main trail continuing straight ahead and to a right-hand turn leading up to Cod Pond, some 0.8 mile away. Continue straight ahead instead of turning right, following signs that point the way to more-distant North Bend and

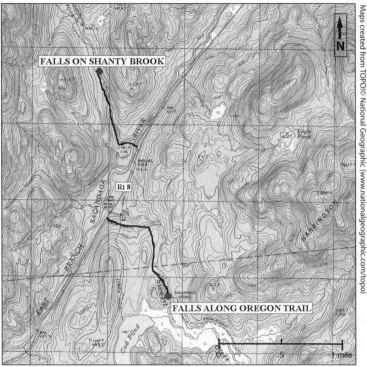

Baldwin Springs. Be prepared for hiking through some marshy areas. In less than 0.7 mile, following what clearly is designed as a snowmobile trail, you will reach the fall.

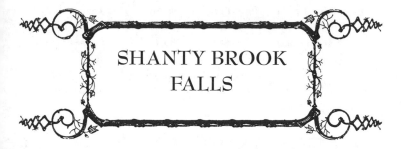

SHANTY BROOK FALLS

Location: Between Wells and Bakers Mills (Warren County)

Accessibility: 1.0-mile hike (one way) over uneven terrain; requires fording the East Branch of the Sacandaga River, so should be attempted only in mid-summer when water levels are low

Difficulty Level: Moderate

Description: This is a very pretty waterfall nestled in the Adirondack wilderness, yet accessible by a 45-minute hike.

Shanty Brook Falls is formed on Shanty Brook, a small stream that rises from Mud Ponds Outlet (to the northwest) and Stockholm Brook (to the north), not too far from the Siamese Pond Wilderness area. A mile or so below the falls, Shanty Brook merges with the East Branch of the Sacandaga River northeast of Shanty Cliffs (which are clearly visible from Rt. 8).

The falls consist of a 12-foot plunge into a small chasm that extends for approximately 500 feet.

What is intriguing about the falls is that instead of the brook coming in straight, at the mouth of the gorge, Shanty Brook approaches from the side so that the west wall at the beginning of the gorge forms the falls. Immediately above the waterfall the stream bed turns north again, leaving the inquisitive mind to marvel at how the brook has been contorted so much.

A short distance above the falls, the stream bed turns into a rock-strewn creek; then, within less than 50 feet, the bedrock protrudes again. It is fascinating to walk across the bedrock and note the etchings, potholes, and tiny cascades that fill its relatively flat surface. McMartin, in her guidebook, *Discover the South Central Adirondacks*, refers to a "mysterious pattern" along the upper section of this part of the creek where a hiker, gifted with a fervent imagination, could attribute the impressions in the rock to a "mythological big-foot." The patterns appear snowshoe-like in shape and are fascinating example of potholes in the making.

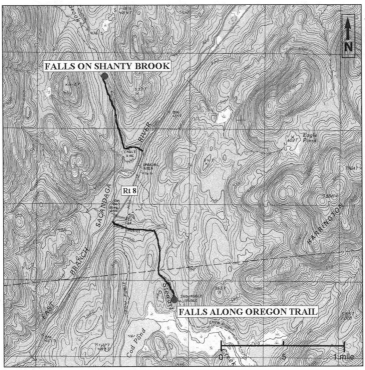

Directions: From Northville proceed north on Rt. 30. Roughly 3.5 miles after leaving Wells, turn right off Rt. 30 onto Rt. 8 and drive northeast for roughly 9.0 miles. Your destination is a large parking lot on the right side of the road. You will pass the county line marker dividing Hamilton and Warren counties 3.1 miles before reaching this point. At 0.5 miles before the parking area, you will pass the third trailhead marker for Cod Pond on the right.

After you have parked, walk north along Rt. 8 for 0.1 mile. Look for a dirt road going off to the left. Follow this dirt road for approximately 50 feet. You will see a pathway leading down the steep embankment to the East Branch of the Sacandaga River, where you are approximately 0.15 mile downstream from the confluence of Shanty Brook with the East Branch.

At this point it is necessary to cross the East Branch. Bear in mind that in the spring or following heavy rainfall, the river may be too high to make fording easy or safe. This hike is best undertaken in mid to late summer when the East Branch becomes shallow and is easily crossed, with many rocks and boulders to step on as you ford the river. Bring along a staff or hiking stick to help maintain balance.

Once across on the other side, the trail continues through the woods for 0.15 mile and then parallels Shanty Brook for the rest of the hike. The hike to the falls from the cable crossing is approximately 0.7 mile going north. Near the end of the hike, look for a small trail that goes off to your right. This leads to the falls, which are approximately 100 yards away. You will see this side trail at a point where you have traversed a particularly boggy section of the trail (but keep in mind that you already will have crossed several boggy sections before reaching this one). If you are visiting in the spring or early summer, keep your ears open. The sound of the waterfall should be audible from the trail to help guide you.

SQUARE FALLS

Location: Between Wells and Bakers Mills (Warren County)

Accessibility: 1.0-mile hike (one way) over uneven terrain: requires fording the East Branch of the Sacandaga River, so should be attempted only in mid-summer when water levels are low

Difficulty Level: Moderate

Description: Square Falls is formed on the East Branch of the Sacandaga River, a medium-sized stream that rises in the hills west of Gore Mountain and merges with the West Branch of the Sacandaga River several miles northeast of Wells.

The waterfall is relatively small—no more than 6 to 7 feet in height—with a fairly flat plateau of bedrock at its top and a deep pool at its base. According to Barbara McMartin in her guidebook, *Discover the South Central Adirondacks*, Square Falls is "formed by a ledge of square-jointed rock" that is reddish in hue. Presumably, this is how the falls came to be named.

What makes this waterfall particularly inviting is the wonderful hike to it, which involves crossing the East Branch of the Sacandaga River, traversing the river's west bank through a deep gorge where there are many scenic overlooks of the stream and its giant boulders, and accessing a fairly remote section of the Adirondacks. According to Walter F. Burmeister in *The Hudson River and its Tributaries*, the gorge "is formed by forest mountain slopes that terrace sharply 718 feet above the right (western) and 615 feet above the left (eastern) shore." After you have hiked along the stream for 30 minutes,

Square Falls seemingly materializes all at once before you in the rocky stream bed, offering numerous ledges and outcroppings of rock above and below the falls for a leisurely picnic lunch.

A tiny chasm channels the water from the base of the falls to a point where the stream bed becomes shallow and rocky again. The deep-cut bedrock below the falls provides an excellent swimming hole. The strata in the riverbed by the falls are tilted nearly vertically. Just above the falls, the riverbed has been cracked into countless, rectangular-shaped sections. Although the metamorphic rock is fairly resistant to erosion and sculpturing, several small potholes in the eastern flank of the falls can be seen.

Square Falls Mountain rises up to the northwest of the stream, but cannot be seen because of the obscuring forest.

A minor cascade less than 3 feet in height can be found directly above Square Falls, and there are several tiny cascades along the

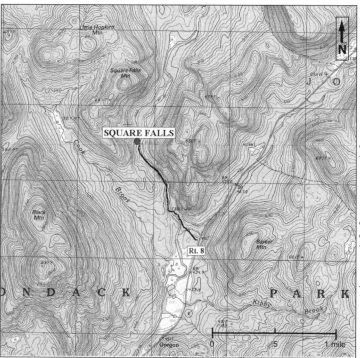

Maps created from TOPO!© National Geographic (www.nationalgeographic.com/topo)

hike in, including one at the cable crossing, but none of any nota-
bility.

Directions: Approximately 3.5 miles north of Wells, turn right off
Rt. 30 onto Rt. 8 and drive northeast for 11.8 miles. En route at
9.4 miles you will pass the second trailhead for Cod Pond on your
right. The parking area for the East Branch Gorge and Square Falls
is 2.4 miles from this point. After 11.5 miles from Rt. 30, you will
cross over Kibby Brook (which is barely noticeable as it comes in
from the east) and then pass by a yellow sign saying "Deer Crossing
Next Two Miles." Guardrails line both sides of the road at this point.
As soon as the guardrails end, pull over into a sandy parking area on
your left and park at the north end of the lot. If you miss the parking area, drive to the trailhead for Siamese Pond, turn around and
drive back on Rt. 8 for 1.9 miles.

From the parking area you will see an old jeep road going
northwest into the woods. Follow it for a short distance, walking no
more than a minute or two. The road turns into a small path as it
veers to the right and leads directly to a tiny brook that rises south
of Eleventh Mountain. Unless you are visiting in early spring or
after a heavy downpour, this brook can be crossed easily. Continue
following the trail as it proceeds west, paralleling the stream. Almost
immediately a small trail goes off to the right and heads up a little
hill. Follow this trail for five minutes as it joins the east bank of the
Sacandaga River and you will come to an area where the river can be
forded. If the waters are high and fording the river looks hazardous,
do not attempt to cross; postpone the trip until drier conditions pre-
vail long enough for the water level to subside. If you visit in mid to
late summer during a dry spell, however, the water level will be very
low and the river can be crossed with ease.

Once you have crossed to the west bank of the Sacandaga River,
follow the river north for less than one mile, proceeding along a fairly discernible trail that goes up and down the sloping west wall of the
gorge as it parallels the stream. You will see the waterfall from afar
several minutes before you reach it. The trail leads directly to the
cascade.

DUNKLEY FALLS

Location: Near Wevertown (Warren County)

Accessibility: Short walk of 0.1 mile (one way) along tote road, fairly even terrain

Difficulty Level: Easy

Description: Dunkley Falls is a small waterfall formed on Mill Creek, a medium-sized stream that rises from Garnet Lake and flows into the Hudson River northwest of The Glen. Although only about 10 feet high, the waterfall is fairly broad and rugged-looking. An enormous boulder rests on the northern bank at the foot of the falls.

About 0.15 mile downstream is the Black Hole, a favorite swimming hole named for its seemingly bottomless depth. The hole is formed in a chasm-like section of the stream along the northern wall where there is much bedrock and several potholes.

The 215 acres of land encompassing both sides of Mill Creek near the falls was recently acquired by the Open Space Institute (OSI) in the town of Johnsburg to ensure the preservation of this land for future generations to enjoy. There are a number of picnic tables and cookeries near the falls.

Directions: From Warrensburg drive north on Rt. 9 and then turn left onto Rt. 28, proceeding northwest. When you reach The Glen—where Rt. 28 crosses over the Hudson River—continue northwest for 2.5 miles. Turn right onto Harrington Road and drive north for 1.8 miles. You will see a pull-off on your right.

Park at this point and walk along an old, abandoned road that parallels the stream for 0.1 mile to the top of the waterfall.

From Wevertown (junction of Rts. 8 & 28) turn right onto Rt. 28 and drive southeast. Turn left onto Harrington Road and drive north for 1.8 miles to the parking area for the falls.

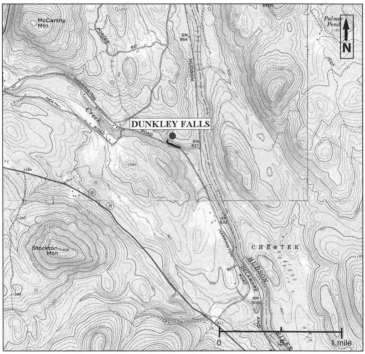

Maps created from TOPO!© National Geographic (www.nationalgeographic.com/topo)

ROUTE 8 WEST

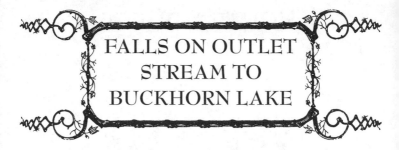

FALLS ON OUTLET STREAM TO BUCKHORN LAKE

Location: Near Piseco Lake (Hamilton County)

Accessibility: 1.3-mile hike (one way) across uneven terrain on well established trail

Difficulty Level: Easy to Moderate

Description: This small cascade is formed on a little creek emanating from Buckhorn Lake (also known in earlier times as Fiddlers Lake). The outlet creek eventually flows into a stream that connects Piseco Lake and Oxbow Lake.

Although the falls are listed on the "The Adirondacks: Central Mountains" topo map, they are fairly obscure and would not be significant except for the fact that they are located on the Northville-Placid Trail, a well-traveled path that spans the distance from Northville to Lake Placid.

The falls consist of a 5-foot cascade formed in a tiny gorge. A footbridge crosses the ravine just upstream from the cascade.

Directions: From Northville take Rt. 30 north to Speculator. At the junction of Rts. 8 & 30 in Speculator, turn left onto Rt. 8 and drive southwest for nine miles. Look for a trailhead marker for the Northville-Placid Trail on your left, and park in an area next to the trailhead.

Follow the blue-blazed trail markers on the Northville-Placid Trail, hiking southeast for roughly 1.3 miles. When you get to a wooden footbridge, you will be able to see the top of the cascade

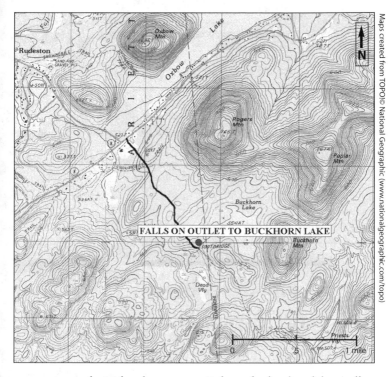

approximately 25 feet downstream. Paths on both sides of the small ravine lead to the bottom of the falls.

To add to the enjoyment of this hike, follow the creek upstream from the falls for 0.2 mile and you will be pleasantly rewarded with excellent scenic views of Buckhorn Lake.

POTHOLERS

Location: North of Knappville (Hamilton County)

Accessibility: 0.1-mile hike (one way) over fairly level terrain

Difficulty Level: Easy

Description: The Potholers are formed on the upper section of East Canada Creek just 0.1 mile upstream from the creek's confluence with Brayhouse Brook. The falls are roughly 15 feet in total height, but rounded and dome-shaped when seen from below. There are no sharp drops, just tiny cascades plunging over rounded bedrock. According to Phil Brown in the *Longstreet Highroad Guide to the New York Adirondacks*, "In spring, when the creek is full, the foaming water resembles a multi-tiered wedding cake."

Numerous potholes, ledges, chutes, and swimming holes have formed where the swirling waters of East Canada Creek have worn away at the reddish-colored, granite bedrock. Just below the falls the stream narrows and passes through a small stricture with huge boulders piled up along the shoreline, and rocks and boulders littering the stream bed.

Near the top of the falls, in contrast, the stream gathers in a small pond and moves along fairly listlessly.

The Potholers derive their name from the numerous, medium-sized, bathtub-shaped potholes in which generations of kids have enjoyed frolicking. According to Adirondack author Bill Ingersoll, the name Potholers was coined by co-author Barbara McMartin's family. The falls are also known as Bray House Falls.

Bray House Falls near Stratford, N. Y.

Potholers got its name from the myriad of naturally formed potholes in the river bed at the falls.

Unlike many of the falls listed in this guidebook, there are no steep banks on either side of the Potholers forming massive shoulders—just fairly flat, forested land not much higher than the falls themselves.

East Canada Creek contains a variety of other interesting waterfalls—including High Falls in Dolgeville, Beardslee's Falls (also known as East Creek Falls) near east Canada lake, and the falls and dam at Ingham Mills—but these are located further downstream near the confluence of East Canada Creek with the Mohawk River.

Directions: At the junction of Rts. 8 & 30 in Speculator, turn left and proceed southwest on Rt. 8. Turn left onto Rt.10 at the junction of Rts. 8 & 10 south of Piseco Lake. After 1.2 miles, turn right onto Piseco Road (also called the Powley-Piseco Road) and drive

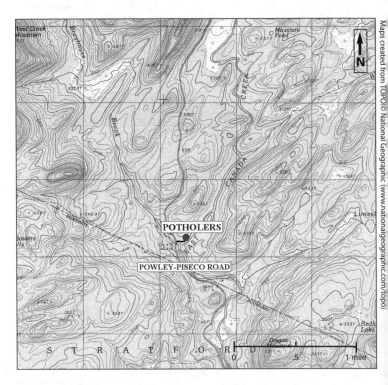

Maps created from TOPO!© National Geographic (www.nationalgeographic.com/topo)

southwest for 10.7 miles. As soon as you come to a small bridge, park to your left.

Follow the north bank of Brayhouse Brook east, going downstream for 0.05 mile almost to its confluence with East Canada Creek. Turn left, following a clearly defined trail that proceeds northward going upstream along the bank of East Canada Creek. Within less than 0.1 mile you will be at the falls.

If you are coming from the Capital District, the best route is to take 1-90 west, and then Rt. 30 to Gloversville. At the intersection of Rts. 30A & 29A, turn left onto Rt. 29A and drive west through the city of Gloversville. Continue northwest on Rt. 29A, going past Peck Lake, Caroga Lake, Canada Lake, Pine Lake, and Pleasant Lake, until you reach the village of Stratford. Turn right onto Mike Smith Road. (Note: if you see Dugway Road, you have gone too far.) After 0.1 mile, Mike Smith Road intersects Piseco Road. Turn right onto Piseco Road and drive north for 7.6 miles. For most of the ride the road will be paved, but the last section consists of hard-packed earth. You will reach a sign that states that the road ahead is open seasonally from May to December. Continue past this sign for 0.2 mile and you will reach a small bridge that spans the terminus of Brayhouse Brook. Park off to your right.

FALLS ALONG
ROUTE 73

The section of Rt. 73 running west to east from Lake Placid to Underwood is the jumping-off point for excursions to a number of waterfalls, including those found near Wilmington Notch, Heart Lake, Keene, Keene Valley, and St. Huberts. For most of its length, Rt. 73 follows the natural contours of the valley, weaving its way from one river valley system to the next.

Beginning in Lake Placid, immediately turn east onto Rt. 86 where the West Branch of the Ausable River races northeast carving out a tremendous mountain pass called Wilmington Notch. There are several notable waterfalls in this area; the best known is the one at High Falls Gorge.

Going southeast on Rt. 73 from Lake Placid, pass over the Chubb River (on which Wanika Falls is to be found) and soon turn south onto Heart Lake Road, which leads for 5 miles into the interior of the Adirondacks. The destination is the Adirondack Loj (an international bed-and-breakfast) and Heart Lake, from which several main trails lead into the heart of the "High Peaks." Although the area is best known for its soaring mountains and vertiginous views, there are also a number of notable waters that can be accessed, including Indian Falls and Rocky Falls.

Continuing east on Rt. 73 past Heart Lake Road, Cascade Mountain quickly comes into view straight ahead. Soon you will enter into a huge pass formed by Pitchoff Mountain to the northwest and Cascade Mountain to the southeast, with the glacially-formed Cascade Lakes directly to the right. During the springtime Cascade Falls is a sight to behold as it drops over 100 feet above the lakes into the valley below.

From here the next 4 to 5 miles take you downhill for a descent of approximately 1000 feet following the tiny brook flowing down from Cascade Lakes to the village of Keene. There are several small waterfalls in this area, including two along the roadside. A larger waterfall, on Styles Brook, unfortunately is not readily accessible to the public.

From Keene it is a drive of 4 miles south to Keene Valley, which, along with trailheads at Heart Lake, the Ausable Mountain Reserve, and Tahawus, constitutes one of the four main entry points into the High Peaks region. This stretch of the road follows the river valley system created by the East Branch of the Ausable River. There are several pretty waterfalls on tributaries of the East Branch just south of Keene Valley, as well as Bushnell Fall on Johns Brook. The flat area by Marcy Airport to the right was once a glacially-fed lake. Phelps Falls, a historically significant waterfall, is nearby, but on private property.

Continuing south on Rt. 73 for several more miles takes you to the St. Huberts region, where there are large parking areas on both sides of the road just before beginning a steep climb up a long hill.

Views from the Adirondack High Peaks.

Hiking the trail from the east side parking area leads to the base of Roaring Brook Falls; hiking southwest along a 0.5-mile private road leads to the Ausable Inn and to trails that follow both sides of the East Branch of the Ausable River to some impressive waterfalls.

Proceeding further southeast on Rt. 73 up the long hill leading out of St. Huberts, you will pass Chapel Pond on the right just after the crest of the hill. You are now driving through a huge mountain pass created by Giant Mountain to the northeast and Round Mountain to the southwest. This area is favored by rock climbers. Observe the great amount of talus by the roadside, proof of nature's periodic violent upheavals.

Continuing southeast, you will parallel the North Fork of the Boquet to the left. There are two waterfalls in this area, one near the roadside and one nearly a mile upstream on the North Fork.

Once you reach Malfunction Junction (the interweaving roads at the junction of Rts. 9 & 73 that were created for the Lake Placid Winter Olympics) you are at the end of the waterfall trip along Rt. 73, with the exception of Split Rock Falls, which is less than three miles northeast on Rt. 9.

WILMINGTON NOTCH

Some of the grandest waterfalls in the Adirondacks are found in
Wilmington Notch.

MONUMENT FALLS

Location: Near Lake Placid (Essex County)

Accessibility: Short walk, less than 0.05 mile from roadside

Difficulty Level: Easy

Description: Monument Falls is formed on the West Branch of the Ausable River, a fairly large stream that rises in the mountains south of North Elba and joins with the East Branch of the Ausable River at Ausable Forks to form the Ausable River.

The view from Monument Falls.

In Bill Healy's *High Peaks of Essex*, Orson (Old Mountain) Phelps is quoted as saying, "The Ausable is the shortest of any river of its volume on the continent. ... No river of its length has so great a number and so great a variety of waterfalls. The number of waterfalls is beyond computation and their variety infinite." So it seemed in the nineteenth century when the wilderness was still largely unexplored.

Monument Falls is located in Wilmington Notch, a narrow mountain gorge that was created by the action of glaciers over 10,000 years ago, pushing out fractured rock from a deep fault zone. The escarpment towers above the river as high as 700 feet to the south and 1700 feet to the north.

Monument Falls is about 5 feet high. What is striking is the setting. Standing near the top of the falls and gazing north, one would be hard pressed to find a more idyllic scene for a photo shoot, for off in the distance stands Whiteface Mountain framed by the river, waterfall, and towering trees.

You may see a number of parked cars when you stop, but don't be overly concerned about finding a crowd at the falls. Almost all of the cars will belong to fishermen, with only a small fraction of them staking out their territory by the falls.

History: The stone cairns by the parking area commemorate the 50th and 100th anniversaries of the State Forest Preserve, serving to remind visitors of the creation of the precious blue line of the Adirondack Park.

Directions: From the south end of Lake Placid village (junction of Rts. 73 & 86), proceed northeast on Rt. 86 towards Wilmington for 4.3 miles. Pull into the parking area on your left. You will see the two, large stone monuments.

Walk downstream along the guard rail for several hundred feet. The falls are off to your left.

HIGH FALLS GORGE

Location: North of Lake Placid (Essex County)

Accessibility: Commercial attraction provides easily negotiated walkways, stairs, and catwalks

Difficulty Level: Easy

Description: There are several waterfalls in the Adirondacks named High Falls. High Falls Gorge, however, is the only commercial attraction so named, and well worth the visit. Thanks to a number of strategically placed catwalks, stairways, and railings, one can safely descend into a deep gorge for close-up views of waterfalls and sculpted rocks.

The falls are formed on the West Branch of the Ausable River, a medium-sized stream. According to C. R. Roseberry in *From Niagara to Montauk*, the main waterfall is 50 feet high and named Climax Falls. The drops and plunges total more than 100 feet of relief over a distance of some 700 feet—hence, the billboard advertisement, which promises "700 feet of falls," referring to distance, not height.

History: Physical proof abounds at High Falls of how the West Branch of the Ausable was at one time more violent and turbulent than it is today. High above the stream bed is a pothole some 7 feet in diameter and over 35 feet deep carved out during the stream's more energetic past.

High Falls Gorge is a commercial attraction featuring one of the
Adirondacks' most spectacular waterfalls.

In the section on High Falls Gorge in *Rocks and Routes of the North County, New York*, Bradford Van Diver describes how waterfalls are formed: "Rivers extend themselves by eroding headway and when they meet a mass of harder rock, falls are formed. Since the rate of erosion under falls is greater than elsewhere, the falls may be viewed as Nature's response to an obstacle placed in its path."

Directions: From the south end of Lake Placid (junctions of Rts. 73 & 86), drive northeast on Rt. 86 for 4.3 miles. You will see Monument Falls to your left. Continue north for another 3.5 miles and you will come to the commercial attraction of High Falls Gorge on your left.

High Falls Gorge is open mid-May through Columbus Day.

FALLS AT
WILMINGTON NOTCH
CAMPGROUNDS

Location: Near Wilmington (Essex County)

Accessibility: 0.1-mile walk (one way) down a steep hill to the top of a deep gorge

Difficulty Level: Easy

Description: This spectacular, 50-foot-high cascade is formed on the West Branch of the Ausable River. The falls are situated at the mouth of a deep, plunging gorge with vertical walls. If you are uneasy about heights, this may not be a hike for you.

The main area for viewing the falls is a rocky promontory that is easily found along the top of the gorge. The falls are safe to view from this vantage as long as one keeps one's distance from the edge of the precipice.

Directions: From High Falls Gorge continue northeast on Rt. 86 for 0.9 mile. The campgrounds are on your left.

From the north the campgrounds are on your right, 1.5 miles southwest of The Flume.

Go to the main building directly in front of the campground's entrance. You will see a map of the campgrounds, which should help orient you. Walk behind the entrance building and the building housing the restrooms will be straight ahead. Proceed to the left side of the restrooms and follow a shallow, rounded gully (which constitutes the path) down a steep hill to the bottom of the slope. In doing so, keep veering to the right and you will end up at the edge of the gorge just downstream from the falls. From here it is easy to find the best lookout for viewing the falls.

The campgrounds are open from the end of April to mid-October. At these times a fee may be required to use the grounds, even if you are only stopping in momentarily to see the falls.

FLUME
FALLS

Location: Near Wilmington (Essex County)

Accessibility: Less than 0.1-mile walk (one way) over variable, uneven terrain

Difficulty Level: Easy

Description: This series of small falls is located in an impressive flume (or narrow canyon) formed on the West Branch of the Ausable River. There are three distinctive waterfalls. One is located near the mouth of the flume just upstream from the bridge spanning the West Branch. The middle fall is located a short distance downstream from the bridge in an area where water is compressed and spews out through a narrow passageway. The third fall is located at the bottom of the flume, with a wonderful swimming hole at its base flanked by steep walls and an abundance of huge boulders.

Donald Morris in the April 1989 issue of *Adirondac Magazine* states that the falls total "60 vertical feet in 200 yards." The flume's narrow, steep walls seem almost like an artificially created channel. It is reminiscent of its northeastern cousin, Ausable Chasm, but on a smaller scale. In *The Adirondacks Illustrated*, Seneca Ray Stoddard describes it as "a natural flume, a long furrow through the rock like the track of a giant plowshare, through which the water shoots like a flash of light."

Directions: From High Falls Gorge continue north along Rt. 86 for another 2 miles or so and you will reach a bridge that spans the

1—Ausable River Looking toward Whiteface Mt., between Lake Placid and Wilmington, N. Y.

The Flume is a miniature version of Ausable Chasm.

West Branch of the Ausable River. Cross over the bridge and park to your left in a large pull-off.

The upper falls can be seen easily from the top of the bridge, looking west towards Whiteface Mountain. The best way to view the two lower falls is to follow the south bank down from the southeast end of the bridge, walking along a well-worn path. It is less than 0.1 mile to the base of the lowest falls.

HEART LAKE
REGION

Directions to Heart Lake: From Lake Placid Village drive southeast on Rt. 73 for approximately 4 miles.

From the village of Keene drive west on Rt. 73 for roughly 11 miles.

Turn south onto Heart Lake Road and continue south for just under 5 miles until you reach the end of the road at the Adirondack

Loj (owned by the Adirondack Mountain Club) by Heart Lake. Park in the area designated for hikers. There is a modest parking fee. Campgrounds are available for overnights.

Rules for the use of the High Peaks Wilderness Area include: bicycles are not allowed; glass beverage containers are not permitted; dogs must be leashed; and day-use hiking parties are restricted to a maximum of 15 people. Park rangers usually are stationed near the trailhead and can provide further information or advise you if permits are required.

Heart Lake is one of four hiking Meccas that leads into the interior of the High Peaks.

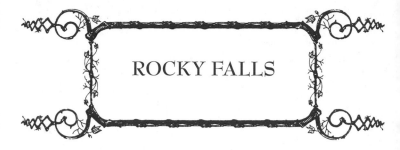

ROCKY FALLS

Location: Near Heart Lake (Essex County)

Accessibility: 2.1-mile hike (one way) over uneven terrain with little change in elevation

Difficulty Level: Moderate

Description: Rocky Falls is a small, but pretty waterfall formed on Indian Pass Brook, a medium-sized stream that rises from Scott Pond and flows into the West Branch of the Ausable River north of Heart Lake.

Rocky Falls is a favorite stopping-off point on the way to Indian Pass.

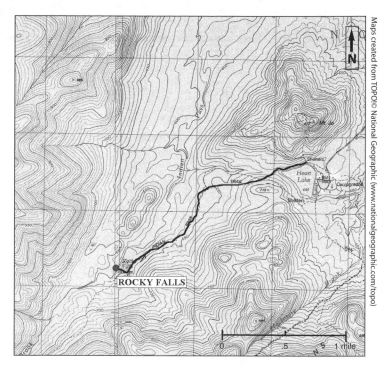

Maps created from TOPO!© National Geographic (www.nationalgeographic.com/topo)

In *The Adirondack Landscape*, author Jerome Wyckoff writes, "Where the dike rock in stream beds is much fractured and eroded, we find waterfalls or rapids—for example, at Rainbow, Indian, Roaring Brook, Rocky, and Bushnell Falls."

The falls are 6 to 8 feet high and formed in a small chasm in the stream bed. Rocky Falls is more of a stopping point to rest and regroup than an impressive waterfall in its own right. It is frequently visited by hikers making their way to and from Indian Pass. There is a lean-to above the falls so that campers may enjoy the serenity of this secluded area. A swimming hole can be found below the falls.

Directions: The trail to Indian Pass and Rocky Falls begins west of the Adirondac Loj, initially following the northwest perimeter of Heart Lake. Look for red-blazed markers. Hike southwest for 2.1 miles and then follow signs that lead off the main trail to the Rocky Falls lean-to and falls.

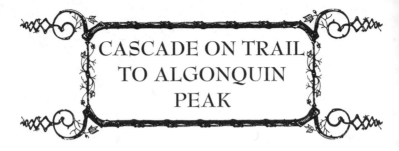

CASCADE ON TRAIL TO ALGONQUIN PEAK

Location: Heart Lake (Essex County)

Accessibility: 2.5-mile hike (one way) with significant gain in elevation

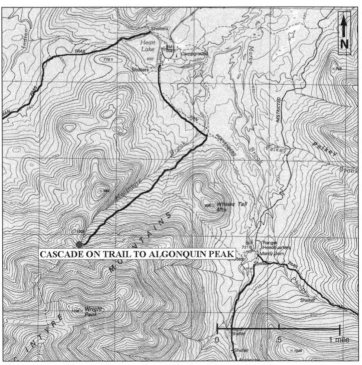

Maps created from TOPO!© National Geographic (www.nationalgeographic.com/topo)

Difficulty Level: Moderate to Difficult

Description: This 15-foot cascade is formed on MacIntyre Brook, a small stream that rises on the northwest shoulder of the MacIntyre Range and flows into Marcy Brook. It is well known to hikers making their way up to Algonquin Peak and Wright Peak.

Directions: From the main parking area at the Adirondack Loj, take the blue-blazed VanHoevenberg Trail south for 0.9 mile to its junction with the Algonquin Peak Trail. Proceed right at the signpost and follow the yellow-blazed Algonquin Peak Trail southwest for 1.5 miles. The waterfall will be on your left just upstream from where the trail crosses a small creek.

INDIAN FALLS

Location: Heart Lake (Essex County)

Accessibility: 4.5-mile hike (one way) over rough terrain, with a nearly 1500-foot gain in elevation

Difficulty Level: Difficult

Description: Indian Falls is formed on Marcy Brook, a small stream that rises on the south slope of Table Top Mountain and flows into the West Branch of the Ausable River northeast of Heart Lake.

Indian Falls provides a natural rest stop on the way to Mt. Marcy, New York State's highest peak.

Indian Falls is a natural rest stop for hikers on their way to the summit of Mt. Marcy, New York State's highest mountain. From the top of Indian Falls there are tremendous views of the MacIntyre Range, including Algonquin Peak, the second highest mountain in the High Peaks.

The waterfall is fairly broad and roughly 25 feet in height. Because hikers emerge directly onto the top of Indian Falls, most are content to sit on the broad expanse of rock and simply enjoy the views. The scramble down to the base of the falls is hardly worth the effort because thickets of bushes and trees press in relentlessly at the bottom, affording no good views.

In *Exploring the 46 Adirondack High Peaks*, James R. Burnside describes the falls: "Here, Marcy Brook sweeps down through a widening clearing and, at the brink of a small precipice, cascades over the chiseled lip of a huge, rounded rock ledge." Since the majority of hikers make the trek up to Mt. Marcy during summer or fall, Marcy Brook is typically seen when it is carrying comparatively less water. Under these circumstances, the top of the falls can look more like a rounded ledge of dry rock with a rivulet going over it. If you want to see the falls in all its glory, go in early spring or following an intense period of rainfall.

History: The name Indian Falls—like Indian Pass, a deep notch between Mt. Marshall and Wallface Mountain, Indian Lake along Rt. 30, and Indian Head, a high bluff overlooking lower Ausable Lake—illustrates the rich Native American history of the area.

According to Sandra Weber in *Mount Marcy: The High Peak of New York*, Indian Falls was first known as Wallace Falls (after Edwin R. Wallace, a guidebook author), and then later as Crystal Falls.

Marcy Brook is probably best known to hikers as the small stream that is impounded 2.1 miles east of Heart Lake to form Marcy Dam, a camping Mecca for hikers. In the late 1800s a lumber dam intercepted the stream, permitting lumberjacks to use controlled releases of water to drive logs down Marcy Brook.

The J. J. Rogers Company of Ausable Forks once maintained a lumber camp next to Indian Falls, serving as an outpost while the surrounding forest was being harvested. The falls also served,

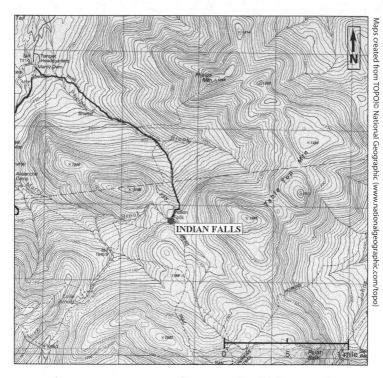

according to one account, as a base camp for the first recorded ski ascent of Mt. Marcy, made by Irving Langmuir, a famous General Electric scientist, and John Apperson.

According to Edith Pilcher in *Up the Lake Road*, the falls were once owned by the Adirondack Mountain Reserve, which purchased over 40,000 acres of land in the High Peaks area of the Ausable Lakes in the late 1800s so that the land wouldn't be further desecrated by lumbering.

Directions: Start at the VanHoevenberg trailhead at the northeastern end of the parking area and hike southeast for 2.1 miles to Marcy Dam. From Marcy Dam continue along the main, blue-blazed trail heading southeast towards Mt. Marcy. Very quickly you will encounter Phelps Brook on your left. After the trail crosses over Phelps Brook, you will notice several small cascades and flumes along the stream, which will now be flowing down on your right. Continue hiking uphill until you reach Indian Falls, some 2.4 miles from Marcy Dam, or a total of 4.5 miles from the Adirondack Loj parking area.

Don't be concerned that you might inadvertently pass the falls without noticing them. The trail crosses right over Marcy Brook, a broad stream that is impossible to miss, especially during the wet season. If Marcy Brook proves difficult to ford, follow a bypass pathway to your right. In less than half a minute you will come to a point where several large boulders permit you cross the stream. The falls are just downstream from this point.

If you are backpacking, bear in mind that camping by the falls is not permitted.

FALLS ON TRIBUTARY TO LAKE COLDEN

Location: Near Heart Lake (Essex County)

Accessibility: 6.0-mile hike (one way) with significant gain in elevation

Difficulty Level: Difficult

Description: This medium-sized waterfall is formed on an unnamed stream that rises on the southern slopes of Algonquin Peak and flows into Lake Colden (elevation 2764 feet).

Avalanche Lake is along the journey to several falls on a small tributary to Lake Colden.

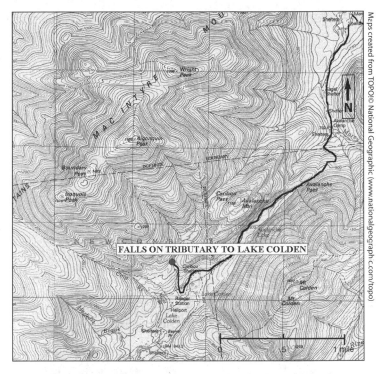

FALLS ON TRIBUTARY TO LAKE COLDEN

Maps created from TOPO!© National Geographic (www.nationalgeograph.com/topo)

The falls are roughly 25 feet high and formed in a rocky chasm that is visible from the trail. Several waterslide cascades are encountered further upstream. About 0.3 mile from Lake Colden, a small cascade can be seen on the way to the falls.

Directions: From the main parking area, follow the blue-blazed VanHoevenberg Trail southeast for 2.1 miles to Marcy Dam. From there follow the yellow-blazed trail leading south to Avalanche Pass. At the south end of Avalanche Lake just before reaching Lake Colden, take the blue-blazed trail southwest leading upwards towards Algonquin Peak. You will reach this point after hiking 3.0 miles from Marcy Dam. At 0.2 mile a small cascade is reached. At 0.8 mile the main waterfall is encountered.

ROUTE 73

WANIKA FALLS

Location: Near Lake Placid (Essex County)

Accessibility: 7.0-mile hike (one way) over variable terrain with little gain in elevation

Difficulty Level: Difficult

Description: Wanika Falls is formed on the Chubb River, a large stream that rises between Street and Nye mountains, and merges with the West Branch of the Ausable River near the Lake Placid airport. The Chubb River is purported to have been named for Joseph Chubb, an early settler in North Elba.

The falls consist of several large cascades. According to Bruce Wadsworth in *An Adirondack Sampler: Day Hikes for All Seasons*, "Here, in a series of drops, water cascades several hundred feet to a pool."

Two smaller cascades are located approximately 1.5 miles further south along the Northville-Placid Trail at a point where the trail crosses over two branches of a brook.

Directions: From Lake Placid go south on Rt. 73, turning right (northwest) onto Old Military Road (Rt. 35) just north of the towering Lake Placid Olympic Ski Jump. From Old Military Road turn left onto Averyville Road (Rt. 23) and drive southwest for 1.1 miles. Park at the designated trailhead area.

The hike to the falls follows the Northville-Lake Placid Trail south for 6.7 miles. Bear in mind that in order to see the cascade,

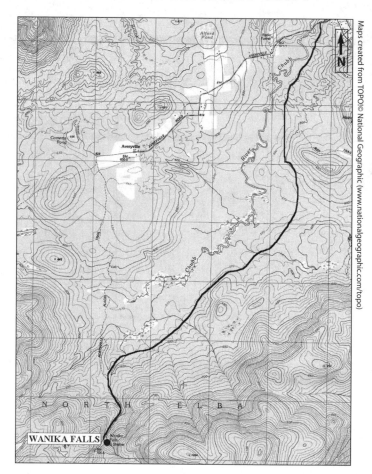

you must cross over to the east bank at the falls, which means fording the stream. If the water level is low, access to the falls is a quick rock-hop across boulders to the opposite bank of the stream. If the water level is high, caution will need to be exercised. The upper fall is approximately 100 yards above the lean-to.

CASCADE LAKE FALLS

Location: Upper Cascade Lake, southeast of Lake Placid (Essex County)

Accessibility: Roadside

Description: This stupendous cascade is formed on Cascade Brook, a small stream that rises on the western shoulder of Cascade Mountain and flows into upper Cascade Lake. The waterfall is over 100 feet high and is best seen in its entirety from Rt. 73, which provides a more distant, all-encompassing perspective. From close up, the fall cannot be viewed as a whole.

If you visit in the summer, there will be little to see because the water relies upon spring snow melt in order to put on a dazzling show.

History: Upper Cascade Lake is located in a deep mountain pass between Cascade Mountain and Pitchoff Mountain. Originally the lake was called Long Pond, which later changed to Edmund's Pond. Around 1878, Nicaner and Edna Miller built a summer hotel between the two lakes, where the distant sound of the roaring falls in the early spring undoubtedly added to the hotel's attraction. The Millers re-christened the lakes "Cascade Lakes." Little evidence remains that a hotel once occupied the wide, open area between the two lakes, but traces of the hotel's old reservoir still exist near the base of the falls, according to Phil Gallo in *By Foot in the Adirondacks*.

There is a widespread notion that the two lakes were once one, and that an avalanche in 1860 divided the lake into two bodies of water. According to Philip G. Terrie, Jr., in the Editor's Introduction to *Peaks and People of the Adirondacks*, the lakes were separated by a narrow neck of land as far back as records go, which is before 1812.

The land between the two lakes was a major source of iron ore in past centuries.

Directions: From Lake Placid (junction of Rts. 86 & 73), take Rt. 73 and proceed southeast for roughly 7 miles. Just past the trailhead to Cascade Mountain and Pitchoff Mountain on your right, you will see Upper Cascade Lake. When you see a tiny isthmus that divides Upper Cascade Lake from Lower Cascade Lake, turn off on a dirt road to the right that leads down to the lake area. Park in the large parking area next to where a summer hotel once stood.

There are excellent views of Cascade Lake Falls from the parking area, the turn-off leading down to the parking area, and along Rt. 73.

Cascade Lake Falls is one of the highest Adirondack waterfalls that can be seen from roadside.

CLIFFORD FALLS

Location: Keene (Essex County)

Accessibility: Roadside

Description: Clifford Falls is formed on Clifford Brook, a small stream that rises near North Notch and flows into the East Branch of the Ausable River several miles north of Keene.

The falls consist of several chutes and drops descending through a carved out section of the creek directly under a picturesque bridge.

Directions: From Keene (northern junction of Rts. 73 and 9N North) there are two approaches that lead to the falls.

Approach #1. Drive northwest on Rt. 73 for 0.7 mile. Turn right onto Alstead Mill Road and continue northwest for another 1.1 miles. When you come to Bartlett Road, turn right and drive north for 0.6 mile. At Clifford Falls Lane turn left, and in 0.5 mile you will reach a small bridge. Park off to the left before crossing the bridge.

Approach #2. Drive north on Rt. 9N for 1.5 miles. Turn left onto Lacy Road, cross over the East Branch of the Ausable River, and continue uphill on Lacy Road (a dirt-packed road) going west. After 2.2 miles you will come to an intersection. Go straight ahead onto Clifford Falls Lane and follow it for 0.5 mile. When you come to a one-lane bridge, park off the road to your left before crossing over the bridge.

The falls are visible from the bridge. Please bear in mind that the land around the bridge is private property, so you must stay on the bridge and road.

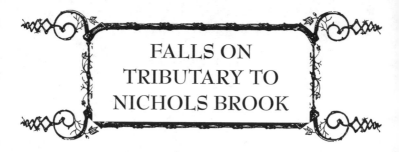

FALLS ON TRIBUTARY TO NICHOLS BROOK

Location: Keene (Essex County)

Accessibility: Less than 1.0-mile hike (one way) following an old, abandoned road with a 200-foot gain in elevation

Difficulty Level: Easy to Moderate

Description: This waterfall is formed on a small, unnamed tributary of Nichols Brook. The tributary develops from rivulets rising on Black Mountain and South Notch, and enters Nichols Brook northeast of a place called Beaver Flow.

In a small glen less than 0.05 mile in length there are two 15-20-foot cascades interspersed with several small cascades.

History: The falls are near the famous Jack Rabbit Trail—named after the Norwegian, Herman "Jack Rabbit" Johannsen, who laid out parts of the original trail between 1916 and 1928.

Directions: From Keene (junction of Rts. 73 & 9N) proceed northwest on Rt. 73 across the East Branch of the Ausable River and drive uphill for 0.7 mile. Turn right onto Alstead Mill Road (formerly Old Military Road) and drive west. You will soon pass the Barkeater Inn and Cross County Ski Center on your right. When you get to Bartlett Road (a dirt road off to your right), Alstead Mill Road suddenly changes from paved to hard-packed dirt. Continue west on Alstead for another 1.8 miles until you come to its end, for a total distance of 3.0 miles from Rt. 73.

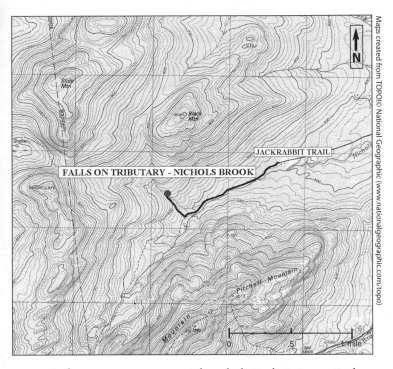

Park in an area opposite Adirondack Rock & River Guide Service. Walk to the western end of the property. You will see the trailhead for the Jack Rabbit Cross County Ski Trail, which is a continuation of Alstead Mill Road. Hike along the Jack Rabbit Trail for a little over 0.8 mile, going southwest. You will see a huge boulder with a smooth, flat surface facing the trail to the right. Immediately after this you will walk across a wooden bridge spanning the small stream containing the waterfalls, which are about 0.2 mile upstream. Hike further west along the Jack Rabbit Trail for no more than 0.1 mile. Just as you reach the point where an expansive vista opens up containing a beaver-created pond framed by rock-faced cliffs on distant hills to the south, yellow trail markers lead to the right. Follow the yellow-blazed trail for 0.1 mile to the falls. The trail leads over the top of a 15-foot cascade into an area of hemlocks and pine needles where you can hike up and down the side of the ravine in order to see the various cascades.

HULLS FALLS

Location: Keene (Essex County)

Accessibility: Roadside

Description: Hulls Falls is formed on the East Branch of the Ausable River, a medium-sized stream that originates from Lower Ausable Lake southwest of Saint Hubert and eventually joins with the West Branch of the Ausable River at Ausable Forks to form the Ausable River.

The waterfall is roughly 20 feet in height and fairly broad and hulking, with many rock outcroppings.

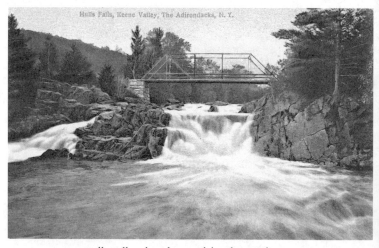

Hulls Falls is broad, powerful and magnificent.

The waterfall is just east of a small tributary known as Hull Basin Brook, which contains a small falls in a narrow rift called Hulls Basin Brook Flume.

Directions: Take Rt. 73 to Keene (northern junction of 9N North and Rt. 73). Nearly opposite from Rt. 9N North, take Hulls Falls Road south and drive uphill for 1.6 miles. You will come to a small bridge that spans the East Branch of the Ausable River. Hulls Falls is directly below and downstream (west) from the bridge, and visible if you walk out onto the bridge.

Remain on the bridge in order to view the waterfall. The land shouldering Hulls Falls is private and posted.

FALLS AT JAY

Location: Jay (Essex County)

Accessibility: Roadside view, with short scramble to stream bed for a closer look

Difficulty Level: Easy

Description: This small, but broad cascade is formed on the East Branch of the Ausable River, a large stream that rises from the Ausable Lakes and joins with the West Branch of the Ausable River at Ausable Forks to form the Ausable River.

Although the total relief is not much greater than 10 feet, the falls are of interest because they consist of a large area of tilted bedrock with many potholes and carved indentations in the stream bed. A huge boulder rests at the top of the falls. Old foundation ruins can be seen next to the cascade along the east bank.

History: In the 1800s Jay was a heavily industrialized village with the Purmont Forge as its centerpiece. Over the ensuing years the village became rural and is now home to *Adirondack Life Magazine*.

A covered bridge was erected in 1857 just downstream from the falls. A new metal bridge took its place in 1997, and the old bridge now rests along the side of the road at the corner of North Jay Road and Glen Road, several hundred feet from its original position.

Directions: From Keene (northern junction of Rts. 73 & 9N) drive north on Rt. 9N for about 10 miles. When you get to Jay, turn right onto Mill Hill Road (opposite the left-hand turn for Rt. 86) and drive southeast, going downhill for 0.2 mile. Cross over a one-lane bridge spanning the East Branch of the Ausable River and park in an area immediately on your right.

The falls are directly below, with a path conveniently leading down from the parking lot to the bedrock and falls.

BUSHNELL FALLS

Location: Near Keene Valley (Essex County)

Accessibility: 5-mile hike (one way), but with a gradual ascent; short bushwhack at the end along stream

Difficulty Level: Difficult

Description: Bushnell Falls is formed on Johns Brook, a medium-sized stream that rises south of Slant Rock (an impressive boulder worthy of a visit in its own right) and flows into the East Branch of the Ausable River at Keene Valley.

The falls are formed in a pretty gorge where the stream drops for 20 feet, cutting through a block of solid rock. It is a place that is secluded and amenable for meditation, and well known in local literature.

History: The waterfall was named by Keene Valley guides after Rev. Horace Bushnell, who made frequent visits to Keene Valley from his home in Hartford, Connecticut. Bushnell enjoyed philosophical discourse and wrote a book entitled *The Moral Uses of Dark Things*.

In *Peaks and People of the Adirondacks*, Russell Carson talks about an evening spent with Dr. Bushnell in which, being asked for an extract for midge and mosquito bites, Bushnell responded, "I confess there is one thing which I cannot account for—that man, who is made in God's image, can be made perfectly miserable by a little creature [indicating on the tip of his forefinger] no bigger than that!" Any visitor to New York's forests and streams will agree that

John's Brook is one of four main inroads into the High Peaks region and a
sure way to get to Bushnell Falls.

Rev. Bushnell's comment rings just as true today as it did back in the late 1800s.

According to Edith Pilcher in *Up the Lake Road*, the falls at one time belonged to the Adirondack Mountain Reserve (AMC), but were sold to New York State in a series of five huge land deals from 1921 to 1932.

Directions: From Rt. 73 in the village of Keene Valley, follow Adirondack Street for 1.6 miles west at the DEC sign "Trails to the High Peaks" until you reach the parking area for "The Garden." If the parking area for The Garden is filled with cars, as it often is, it may be necessary to drive back down to the village, park there, and return by foot or catch a shuttle.

The Garden is a main route into the High Peaks, and certain rules have been established to keep the High Peaks Wilderness from becoming over-used: bicycles are not allowed; glass beverage con-

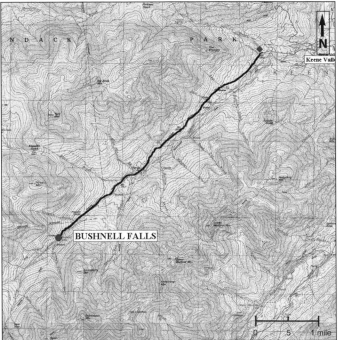

BUSHNELL FALLS

tainers are not permitted; dogs must be leashed; and day-use hiking parties are restricted to a maximum of 15 people.

Follow the main, yellow-blazed trail paralleling Johns Brook and continue southwest for five miles. You will pass by Johns Brook Lodge, a small, rustic bed & breakfast for hikers heading into the interior of the High Peaks region. Although the hike may be time consuming, the trail itself is not very demanding and ascends gradually as you follow Johns Brook. The trick is in knowing where to look for the falls. The last trail marker, indicating that Bushnell Falls is only 0.15 mile away, can be deceiving. When you follow the trail downhill to Johns Brook, you won't come out at Bushnell Falls. You will find, instead, a flat, rocky area of creek bed, both upstream and downstream. To get to Bushnell Falls, follow Johns Brook downstream for less than 0.1 mile. Be prepared for a combination bushwhack and rock hop. The *High Peak Region: Guide to the Adirondack Trails* states that "a vague spur trail left leads 250 yards, very steeply, down to the base of the falls." Stay next to the stream and you can't get lost.

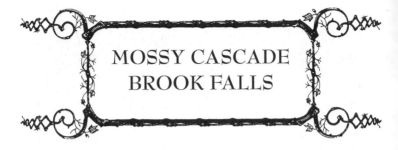

MOSSY CASCADE BROOK FALLS

Location: Near Keene Valley (Essex County)

Accessibility: 0.8-mile hike (one way) over variable terrain with nearly a 400-foot gain in elevation; last 0.05 mile requires some scrambling to get to falls

Difficulty Level: Moderate

Description: Mossy Cascade is formed on Mossy Cascade Brook, a small stream that rises on the south shoulder of Hopkins Mountain and flows into the East Branch of the Ausable River north of St. Huberts.

The falls are approached by hiking into a narrow ravine, which deepens the further in one proceeds, turning into a box canyon. The first waterfall encountered is an 8-foot-high cascade that can be bypassed easily by continuing along a little trail at the bottom of the ravine. Just a short distance past this cascade is the main waterfall, which descends curtain-like over a dark wall of rock approximately 40 feet high.

In *Discover the Northeastern Adirondacks* by Dennis Conroy, James C. Dawson, & Barbara McMartin, the falls are described as follows: "Some waterfalls emit a sense of power and force. Mossy Cascade is veil-like and dainty. You feel peace here and want to stay—except that it is apt to be damp and chilly in the deep shade." That is an apt description of the falls during the dog days of summer, but like all waterfalls in the early spring, Mossy Cascade Brook Falls can put on quite a show following snow melt.

Mossy Cascade Brook Falls is 40 feet of falling, frolicking water.

While appropriately named in this case, Mossy Cascade also could be the title for many waterfalls in the Adirondacks; the High Peaks contain a myriad of deep glens with lush growth, green moss, and unnamed cascades.

Directions: From the village of Keene Valley, drive south on Rt. 73 for about 2 miles. As soon as you cross over a bridge spanning the East Branch of the Ausable River, pull over into a small parking area on your left.

Next to the southeast end of the bridge, you will see a small sign: "Hopkins—Mossy Cascade." Follow the path leading from this sign. The path parallels the East Branch of the Ausable River for 0.3 mile going northeast. From there the trail is clearly marked as you continue along tote roads, now going east, and then onto a trail that proceeds uphill next to Mossy Cascade Brook. As you approach

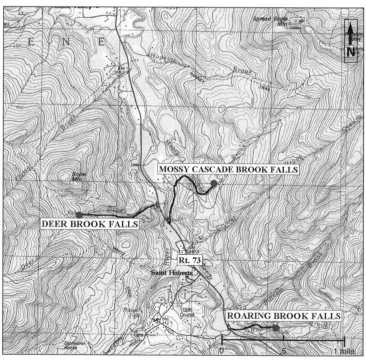

Maps created from TOPO!© National Geographic (www.nationalgeographic.com/topo)

the ravine where Mossy Cascade is located, you will see a small sign pointing the way to the falls. From there you follow the stream up through the ravine for less than 0.05 mile. Be prepared for some rock scrambling. The total hiking distance is 0.8 mile.

The trail ultimately leads up to the summit of Hopkins Mountain.

For those who prefer to avoid entering the ravine, continue uphill along the main trail to the top of the falls, cross over the stream, and make your way around the ravine's rim until you are looking head-on at the falls.

DEER BROOK FALLS

Location: Keene Valley (Essex County)

Accessibility: 1.0-mile hike (one way) over variable terrain with over 500-foot gain in elevation

Difficulty Level: Through gorge—Difficult; bypassing gorge—Moderate

Description: Deer Brook Falls is formed on Deer Brook, a small stream that rises on the south shoulder of Hedgehog Mountain and flows into the East Branch of the Ausable River.

The main waterfall is over 80 feet high and is a wonderful place to rest and cool off as one proceeds up to the overlooks on Snow Mountain. There is a significant amount of talus at the base of the falls, as well as debris from fallen trees and loosened bushes, which the stream evidently is not powerful enough to wash away.

You will encounter several cascades along the hike before reaching Deer Brook Falls. During the first 0.5-0.6-mile hike through the gorge, you will pass by the highest density of small falls and cascades of any stream in this part of the High Peaks region. One often overlaps the next, and the waterfalls are literally too numerous to list.

Near the end of the gorge just before the path climbs uphill and joins the main trail, there is a rock cave on the right.

When you reach the footbridge crossing over Deer Brook, there is a double cascade under and down from the bridge, as well as two large potholes—large tubs with running water that have assuredly cooled off many overheated hikers during the dog days of summer.

Just upstream from the footbridge is a 30-foot waterfall coming into Deer Brook from a small tributary that the Snow Mt./Roostercomb Trail parallels as it continues uphill, as well as an 8-foot cascade on Deer Brook itself.

Directions: From the village of Keene Valley, drive south for approximately 2 miles and park at the northwest end of the bridge crossing the East Branch of the Ausable River.

The hike starts at the trailhead for Snow Mt./Roostercomb Mountain, just 0.05 mile northwest of the bridge. The trail begins with an easy, 0.05-mile hike up to a small bridge leading to a private home, followed by a rock scramble of 0.5 mile west through a deep gorge carved out by Deer Brook. If you find the going too difficult, you can always return to the beginning of the gorge (at the pri-

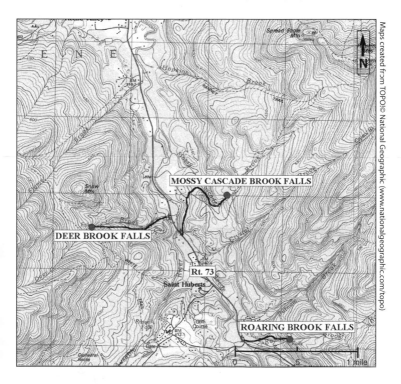

vate road) and take the High Water Route up the winding dirt road on the south side of the stream to where the road veers sharply to the left and the main trail begins. This route also involves a hike of over 0.5 mile. If you follow the trail through the gorge, you will need to be prepared to cross the stream multiple times and to do some rock scrambling. The trail ultimately comes up the side of the gorge and joins the main trail, less than 0.1 mile from where the main trail comes up from the dirt road. When you finally reach the point where a footbridge crosses Deer Brook, you will see a sign pointing the way to Deer Brook Falls. The falls are a scant 0.1 mile further upstream. If you look closely, you can see the falls from the footbridge. Stay on the south side of the stream and follow an easy trail for the rest of the distance.

ROARING BROOK FALLS

Location: Keene Valley (Essex County)

Accessibility: 0.4-mile hike (one way) with little elevation change

Difficulty Level: Easy

Description: The highest waterfall visible from roadside in the Adirondacks is Roaring Brook Falls. The cascade is formed on Roaring Brook, a small stream that rises on the western cirque of Giant Mountain and flows into the East Branch of the Ausable River after joining up with a brook issuing from the outlet at Chapel Pond.

According to John Winkler in *A Bushwhacker's View of the Adirondacks*, Roaring Brook Falls possesses a total height of 290 feet, with an upper drop of 180 feet and a lower drop of 110 feet. Edith Pilcher, in *Up the Lake Road*, assesses the height of the falls at 325 feet. In *Exploring the 46 Adirondack High Peaks*, James R. Burnside describes Roaring Brook Falls as "a 325 foot waterfall that prompts people to stop and stare from the highway. During most of the year, excluding the spring run off, the flow is slim and wispy." Wallace Bruce, a nineteenth-century author, wrote in *The Hudson* that Roaring Brook Falls is "some four hundred feet high, a very beautiful waterfall in the evening twilight."

As if that weren't enough, Seneca Ray Stoddard had this to say in *The Adirondacks Illustrated*: "There [is] Roaring Brook Falls, the highest in the mountains; nearly 200 feet sheer fall at one leap, and I tell you it isn't much besides spray when it reaches the bottom."

Obviously, visual estimates of height can vary considerably from one author to another.

From Rt. 73 the two drops appear to be one. A further highlight of the falls is that it drops into what geologists call a hanging valley, where a glacially-created tributary enters a main valley system.

History: Even peace-loving cascades like Roaring Brook Falls can be temperamental at times. On June 29, 1963, a sudden deluge of 6 inches of rain in one and a half hours set into motion a huge 15-foot-high mudslide that raced down the valley of Roaring Brook Falls and out across Rt. 73.

Directions: From Keene Valley drive south along Rt. 73 for about 3 miles until you come to a left-hand turn opposite the second

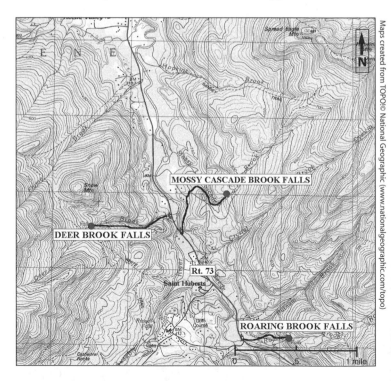

right-hand turn leading up to the Ausable Club. Turn left and into the parking area for Giant Mountain and Roaring Brook Falls.

Coming from the southeast, continue north on Rt. 73. As soon as you reach Chapel Pond on your left, you will start descending a long, steep hill. At the bottom of the hill—1.3 miles from Chapel Pond—pull into a parking area on your right.

Follow the well-worn trail north for slightly less than 0.4 mile to the base of the falls.

To get a safe, panoramic view of Roaring Brook Falls without leaving the roadside, continue driving east on Rt. 73 from the parking area for Roaring Brook Falls, proceeding steadily uphill. Look for a pull-off on your left. From here there are excellent views of Roaring Brook Falls in the distance.

FALLS ON NORTH FORK OF THE BOQUET RIVER, #1 & #2

FALLS #1

Location: Near St. Huberts (Essex County)

Accessibility: 0.8-mile hike (one way) over varied terrain with only 100 feet in elevation gain

Difficulty Level: Moderate; the last 0.2 mile of trail has been eroded in places by the stream

Description: These falls are formed on the North Fork of the Boquet River, a medium-sized stream that rises between Dix and Dial Mountains and joins with the South Fork of the Boquet River at Euba Mills. The Boquet has the distinction of being the steepest river in New York State, dropping over 3200 feet before entering Lake Champlain at an elevation of 95 feet.

The falls are not particularly high—perhaps 20 feet altogether—with the tallest single drop probably no greater than 8 feet—but they appear massive because of the amount of exposed bedrock. Huge slabs of rock are everywhere.

A wonderful swimming hole, created by a large, deep rectangular fissure in the bedrock, can be found at the base of the main falls.

History: The waters of the North Fork of the Boquet once provided power to nearby Euba Mills, a bustling mill town whose heyday was in the late nineteenth century. In 1903, however, the entire community—homesteads, a schoolhouse, blacksmith shop, and

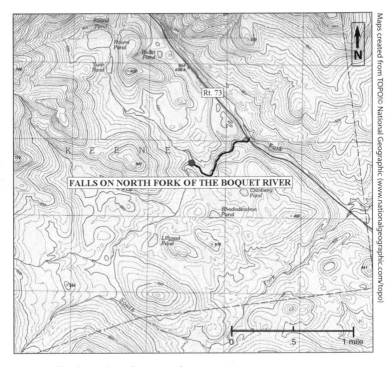

FALLS ON NORTH FORK OF THE BOQUET RIVER

Rt. 73

Maps created from TOPO!© National Geographic (www.nationalgeographic.com/topo)

sawmill—burned to the ground.

The origin of the name Boquet (pronounced *Bow-kwet*) is disputed. Alec C. Proskine in *No Two Rivers Alike* states that the river was named after a French missionary, Charles Boquet. In *Historical Sketches of Northeastern New York and the Adirondack Wilderness*, Nathaniel Sylvester speculates that the name either arose from the bright wild flowers adorning the river's bank (a hypothesis put forward by William Gilliland, an early settler in Elizabethtown, as well), or was derived from the French word *boquet*, for "trough," which sections of the river do resemble.

Directions: From the easternmost road leading to the Ausable Club, opposite the trailhead parking for Roaring Brook Falls, continue southeast on Rt. 73 for about 4 miles. Approximately 1.5 miles before you arrive at the junction of Rts. 9 & 73, you will reach a small bridge that crosses over the North Fork of the Boquet. Park on the opposite side of the road at a pull-off or in one of two, small, off-road parking areas that are located on either side of the river.

From the east side of the bridge, follow the river upstream for 50 feet to a small parking area. This is where the (unmarked) trail begins. The first 0.7 mile of the trail is easy to negotiate as you follow the stream southwest. You will eventually come to a large area of exposed bedrock next to the stream. Just past this area, the stream suddenly veers northwest. The waterfall is over 0.2 mile upstream from this bend. The trail continues to follow the base of the ravine, but the hiking is much more demanding because the trail has been heavily eroded along the stream's edge. You can follow this eroded trail or you can take a steep trail up to the top of the ravine and then follow a faint path northwest as it parallels the stream, eventually leading back down to the North Fork downstream from the falls. Either way, you will arrive at the base of the falls.

FALLS # 2

Location: Near St. Huberts (Essex County)

Accessibility: 50-foot downhill scramble to stream bed

Difficulty Level: Easy

Description: This gorgeous flume-like falls is formed in a narrow chasm where the North Fork of the Boquet River drops about 8 feet. The erosive power of the stream is evidenced everywhere at the top of falls, where a multitude of potholes can be seen.

Directions: Follow the directions given to the parking area for Falls #1. Go to the northeast end of the bridge, walk 50 feet east along the guard-rail, then follow an obvious path to your left that leads down to the stream below, where the North Fork now parallels Rt. 73.

It is possible to glimpse the falls from Rt. 73 as you drive west from the junction of Rts. 9 & 73 towards St. Huberts; however, there are no pull-offs, so a passing glance is all that can be obtained.

SPLIT ROCK FALLS

Location: South of Elizabethtown (Essex County)

Accessibility: Near roadside

Difficulty Level: Easy

Description: Split Rock Falls is formed on the Boquet River, a medium-sized stream that rises near the Dix Mountain Range and flows into Lake Champlain at Willsboro. The falls are roughly 30 feet high and consist of 3 plunges and 2 pools.

History: Split Rock Falls has been visited since the days of early Native Americans, who believed that the spirit of a dead chief haunted the rocks and that his spirit could be placated only by throwing gifts out onto the water. In later years the falls served as a territorial line between the Mohawks and Algonquins. In 1713 the Treaty of Utrecht established the waterfall as the northern limit of British domination. From 1763 until 1777, the falls represented the boundary between New York and Canada. Split Rock Falls has served other purposes than just as a boundary line, however. In 1825 Basil Bishop built an iron forge at the base of the falls. Using a special kind of forge called a *trompe,* he created wind to fan the fire by forcing water through a vertical tube. Bishop also used the power of falling water to drive a trip hammer and, in this fashion, made iron brooms.

In 1982 the property was bequeathed to the State of New York by the family of Richard W. Lawrence. Little trace of the industrial past remains.

Split Rock Falls is one of the prettiest and most accessible waterfalls in the Adirondacks. During high waters, it can also be one of the deadliest.

Directions: From the junction of Rts. 73 & 9 several miles west of the Adirondack Northway, proceed north on Rt. 9 for 2.3 miles. As soon as you cross over the Boquet River, pull into a designated parking area on your right. There are several paths leading off from the parking lot to the base and top of the falls.

EAST BRANCH OF THE AUSABLE RIVER

Accessibility: 10.0-mile hike (roundtrip) over variable terrain

Difficulty Level: Difficult

Ausable Lake—lake source of the Ausable River and powerhouse of its mighty waterfalls.

Nestled in the St. Huberts region of the Adirondack Mountains is a wonderful, ten-mile hike past a series of stunning waterfalls, including Rainbow Falls, Beaver Meadow Falls, Wedge Brook Falls, Pyramid Falls, Artists Falls, and several smaller falls. The hike follows along the East Branch of the Ausable River, which races over a dam at the north end of Lower Ausable Lake, past the Ausable Club (privately owned by the Adirondack Mountain Reserve), and down through Keene Valley. As one hikes along this system of interconnecting trails, one passes between the Great Range (Sawteeth, Gothics, Armstrong, the Wolfjaw Mountains, etc.) to the west, and Noonmark Mountain, Bear Den Mountain, Dial Mountain, Nippletop, and Mount Colvin, to the east.

The East Branch of the Ausable is a fast-flowing, highly energetic stream that, along with the West Branch, drains nearly one-quarter of the High Peaks region. Along its course the Ausable and its tributaries produce some very striking waterfalls, not just in the St. Huberts region, but also further downstream at High Falls in Wilmington and Rainbow Falls at Ausable Chasm.

The hike begins at the Ausable Club's St. Huberts Inn, a Victorian structure built in 1890. This entire hike is on private lands of the Adirondack Mountain Reserve (AMR). Public access to these trails is accorded through an easement granted by the AMR in 1978. Hikers must observe prohibitions against camping, fishing, hunting, and off-trail travel, and no dogs are permitted in this game reserve.

It helps to have a mental map of the hiking terrain you will be traversing. Picture two long mountain ridges forming a deep, fairly broad valley. The East Branch of the Ausable River runs between them in a relatively straight line, flowing northeast from Lower Ausable Lake down to and past the Ausable Club. Two hiking trails parallel the river—the West River Trail following the west bank, and the East River Trail following the east bank—as well as Lake Road, which is further east from the East River Trail. Although Lake Road may be more expedient than either of the two river trails, bear in mind that it affords no views of the Ausable River, and thus should be taken only if covering many miles quickly is the principal goal.

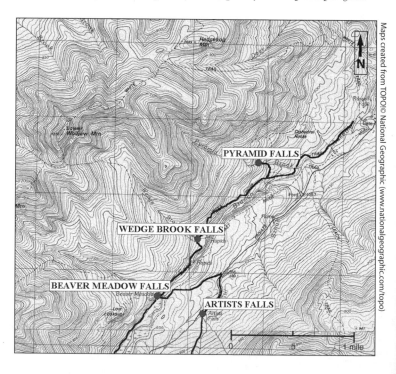

Giant Mountain as seen from the Ausable Club near the start of the
waterfall trail.

Also take note that the AMR will be changing the name of Lake
Road to Lake Trail to underscore the fact that the road now is used
only for walking.

Directions: To get to the Ausable Club from Keene Valley, take Rt.
73 southeast for several miles and turn right onto the second road
to the Ausable Club Road, opposite the parking area for Roaring
Brook Falls and Giant Mountain. From the Adirondack Northway
(I-87) take Rt. 73 northwest for roughly 7 miles. Turn left onto
Ausable Club Road after driving down a long, steep hill. Park immediately on your left in a designated parking area. Parking is prohibited further up the road or at the Ausable Club unless you are a
member.

From the parking area hike up the road to the Ausable Club, a
distance of about 0.6 mile, and turn left at St. Huberts Inn. Within
several hundred yards you will arrive at an impressive wooden gate
where a dirt-packed, unimproved road known as Lake Road (constructed in 1887) continues for 3.5 miles further, gradually winding its way up to Lower Ausable Lake.

To begin the hike, proceed to the West River Trail. This will
require crossing the Ausable River on a footbridge. Depending upon

the severity of spring's snow melt, which has the potential for heavy flooding, one or more of the footbridges may be out of commission (as were two of them when I last hiked the trails).

The first footbridge can be found by turning right approximately 120 feet in front of the Lake Road gate, where the watchman's hut is located, and following a side road for a short distance as it bears slightly right. When you see a path going off to your left, follow it down to and across the river to the West River Trail.

Another route involves taking the East River Trail, which starts 0.3 mile past the gate from Lake Road, and following it for 0.2 mile until you reach the second footbridge spanning the Ausable over to the West River Trail. If this footbridge has been washed out also, follow the East River Trail for roughly 0.7 mile more and cross over at a place known as The Canyon.

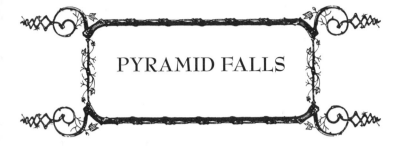

PYRAMID FALLS

Description: Pyramid Falls is formed on Pyramid Brook, a small stream that rises in the hills between Lower Wolfjaw and Hedgehog Mountains and constitutes just one of many little tributaries that flow into the East Branch of the Ausable River.

The main falls are formed at a point where the stream sudden-

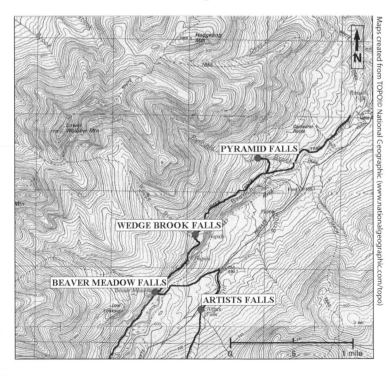

Maps created from TOPO!© National Geographic (www.nationalgeographic.com/topo)

ly alters its course, turning perpendicularly, and flows over a smooth wall of inclined rock that looks very much like the side of a pyramid, dropping some 20 feet. Because of the way the waters are released at the top, the falls also form a triangular, or pyramidal, shape. A smaller, funnel-shaped, 15-foot falls can be seen directly below the main cascade.

Directions: Start the hike from the beginning of the West River Trail at the point where the W. A. White Trail veers off to the right and proceeds up towards Lower Wolfjaw Mountain, and hike upstream along the Ausable River proceeding southwest for a little under one mile. You will pass by the first turn-off for Cathedral Rocks. When you reach the second marker for Cathedral Rocks, which also happens to be the direct route to Pyramid Brook, turn right and hike uphill for slightly over 0.2 mile to Pyramid Falls.

WEDGE BROOK FALLS

Description: Wedge Brook Falls is formed on a small stream that rises on the shoulder of Lower Wolfjaw Mountain and flows into the East Branch of the Ausable River. Wedge Brook contains three pretty falls, all within a short distance of one another. The most distinctive of the three cascades is the middle one, where a small, log foot-

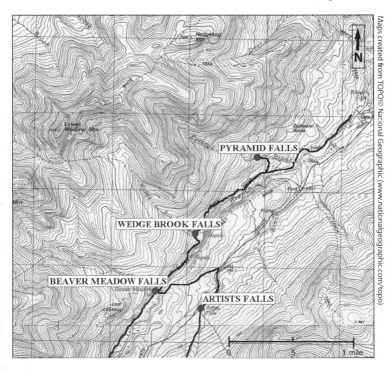

bridge crosses under its base allowing hikers to cross the stream. This 8-foot-high waterfall is a miniature version of Bash Bish Falls in Copake, with the plunging water cleft into two rivulets by a protruding rock. No doubt this wedge-shaped rock inspired the brook's name.

To view the largest of the three falls, which is approximately 30 feet high, cross over the brook and follow Lower Wolfjaw Trail, paralleling the stream uphill for several hundred feet, and then scamper down to the base of the falls.

Directions: From Pyramid Falls return to the West River Trail and continue hiking southwest. Within several hundred feet from the Pyramid Brook/Cathedral Rocks Trailhead, you will come to a cross-over to the east side of the Ausable River via a deep ravine called The Canyon. (If the first two footbridges are unusable, this may be your initial point of crossing from the East River Trail over to the West River Trail.) Continue south on the West River Trail. Roughly 1.5 miles from Pyramid Falls you will reach an overlook of the gorge with the river now far below. A distant, medium-sized waterfall can be seen. This is a scene worth pausing to enjoy. After another 0.3 mile you will arrive at Wedge Brook Falls.

INTERIM

From Wedge Brook Falls continue on the West River Trail for roughly 0.2 mile. You will hike past a section of flumes where the water becomes compressed and greatly accelerated. After another 0.1-0.2 mile you will see a 20-foot-high waterfall off to your left whose upper section is readily accessible from the main trail.

BEAVER MEADOW FALLS

Description: Beaver Meadow Falls is formed on a small stream that rises between Armstrong and Upper Wolfjaw Mountains and flows into the East Branch of the Ausable River a short distance from the base of the falls. The falls have been described as "bridal veil" in appearance, and are certainly striking, for the stream falls from a

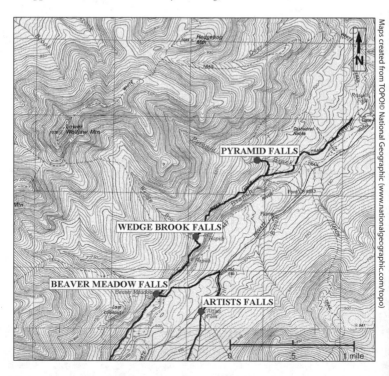

Beaver Meadow Falls is one of the Adirondacks' most photographed
waterfalls.

height of 60 feet and drops nearly vertically onto the rocks below producing an array of secondary chutes and cascades, like fireworks exploding in the night sky.

The top of the falls can be reached by climbing up the Lost Lookout Trail (which begins just south of the falls where a large wooden ladder is visible) for a couple of hundred vertical feet, and then taking a fairly well defined side path to the right. Please remember, however, that waterfalls generally are best appreciated when viewed from their base, often making a trip to the top disappointing and superfluous. If you decide not to heed this advice, exercise caution at the top and do not go too close to the edge. Slipperiness and sloping rocks have lured many a curious, incautious hiker to a sudden death.

Several smaller cascades can be observed in the stream bed above the main falls and should be on your itinerary if you do make the effort to reach the top of the falls.

Directions: Roughly 0.7 mile from Wedge Brook Falls, the West Bank Trail leads directly to and across the base of Beaver Meadow Falls.

RAINBOW FALLS

Description: Rainbow Falls is arguably the most spectacular of the waterfalls on the East Branch's tributaries. It is formed on Rainbow Brook, a small stream that rises on the east flank of Gothics Mountain. This falls should not be confused with another waterfall known as Rainbow Falls that is also on the Ausable River, but at the head of Ausable Chasm.

Rainbow Falls is located in a deep and wild-looking ravine with many boulders strewn about. The falls are close to 150 feet high and consist of a nearly straight plunge down a rocky wall. Jerome Wyckoff in *The Adirondack Landscape* states that "Rainbow Falls is one of many Adirondack waterfalls that have formed in dikes."

Rainbow Falls received its name from the prism of color that often can be seen near the top of the falls when the lighting is just right on a sunny day.

The falls were written up quite eloquently in *The Adirondacks Illustrated* by Seneca Ray Stoddard, the nineteenth-century Adirondack writer, photographer, cartographer, and historian. "We crossed the outlet and went up into the cleft mountain side, very like Ausable Chasm and probably with a like origin. It extends only a short distance but is very beautiful, the gray sides perpendicular for something over a hundred feet, while huge rough boulders fill the bottom, and over the edge of the wall at the north is the Fall, a skein of amber silk that flutters along down the rocks as snow-flake falls and white as clean wool, where, gathering its tiny drops together, it goes softly singing down its emerald-paved steps to the river below."

In more recent times, Clyde H. Smith wrote in *The Adirondacks*: "Rainbow Falls plummets down a 150-foot cliff into a narrow

Rainbow Falls is a 150-foot cascade into a deep box canyon.

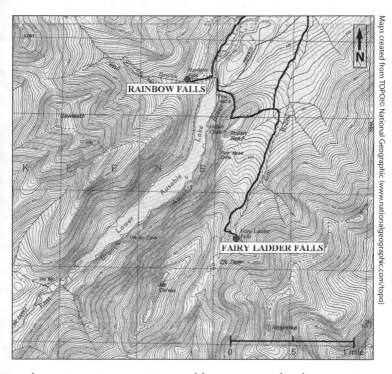

chasm. In spring, vapor generated by its gigantic thundering pours from the grotto like a small rainstorm."

Not surprisingly, the falls are visited during all seasons and for all kinds of reasons. Ice climbing in the winter has become increasingly popular in the Adirondacks, with Rainbow Fall's 150-foot precipice of ice proving irresistible to some adventurers. The first recorded ice climb up Rainbow Falls, according to *Adirondack High Peaks and the Forty-sixers*, occurred when David Bernays scaled the falls in 1952 by cutting steps in the ice wall's center. Climbers should take note, however, that ice climbing at Rainbow Falls now is prohibited by the AMR.

Directions: From Beaver Meadow Falls continue south along the West River Trail for one mile to the Lower Ausable Lake bridge and dam. From this junction, follow the Sawteeth Trail uphill for 0.1

mile. Turn right at the turn-off for Rainbow Falls and follow the trail in for roughly 0.05 mile to the falls.

The falls also can be seen from two other excellent vantage points. One is 0.2 mile up the south end of the Lost Lookout Trail, which diverges from the West River Trail just before the Lower Lake Dam. The other is 0.2 mile up the Gothics Trail to a lookout that is even with the top of the falls, where a sign proffers advice to be heeded by all waterfall viewers: "Don't be a dropout. Stay back from edge."

From Rainbow Falls it is only a short climb up to the ramparts of Indian Head, a 750-foot-high cliff that overlooks Lower Ausable Lake, providing a commanding view of the lake whose waters power the numerous smaller cascades and rapids you have passed on your hike up the West River Trail.

INTERIM

Return to the West River Trail and cross over the foot-bridge below the dam at Lower Ausable Lake so that you end up on the east bank of the East Branch. According to Laura Vicome in her article "Violence in the Valley" in the *2001 Collectors Issue of Adirondack Life* (Vol. XXXII #27), torrential rains in 1856, possibly combined with a mudslide, caused the Wells Dam on the lower Ausable Lake to give way, sending a wall of water down into the valley. Eleven people drowned, and property and crops were destroyed.

Walk back along the Lake Road or, for a more adventurous route, follow the East River Trail downstream (northeast) for 3.5 miles. By hiking along the East River Trail, you will be rewarded at 1.6 miles with a stunning view of a 20-foot waterfall crashing into a wild, rugged gorge. Additional falls await as you continue along the river, with all the falls and flumes now in reverse order from when you initially viewed them on the West River Trail. Unfortunately the East River Trail keeps you so high above the river for the next mile or so—literally clinging to the side of the gorge—that you are more apt to hear the cascades than to see them.

If you prefer to visit several new waterfalls, leave the East River trail at 1.3 miles from Lower Ausable Lake and take a designated "To the Road" side path to Lake Road. When you reach the Lake Road, turn right (back-tracking southwest) for several hundred feet and then follow the Gill Brook Trail, which parallels Gill Brook on your left.

ARTISTS FALLS

Description: Artists Falls is formed on Gill Brook, a medium-sized stream that rises northeast of Nippletop and flows into the East Branch of the Ausable River about 0.8 mile upstream from the Ausable Club. The falls are roughly 20 feet high and formed in a tiny gorge.

Artists Falls was visited by many nineteenth-century artists—including Winslow Homer, Rosewell M. Shurtleff, and many from the Hudson River School—thus acquiring its name.

There are several pretty falls just a short distance upstream.

Gill Brook plays host to a number of waterfalls

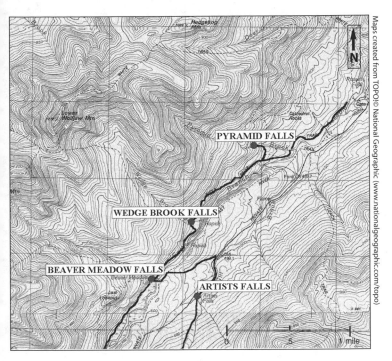

Directions: Proceed upstream on the Gill Brook Trail for 0.4 mile and you will reach the first falls—a broad block of rock about 15 feet high with water cascading over just a small part of it. A short distance further upstream you will come to a long chute-like falls.

At roughly 0.5 mile the trail takes you down and through a tiny gorge that has created a 20-foot-high cascade. This is Artists Falls.

If you continue further upstream, you will pass by two flume falls (one approximately 15 feet high), a small 8 to 10-foot cascade, a fairly striking, highly inclined 25-foot waterfall, another flume waterfall, and a long slide falls. Finally, after another 0.2 mile of agitated waters, you will come to a pretty 10-foot waterfall with a pool at its base. A trail, which leads "To the Road," comes in oblique-ly on the right. This is the turn-around point. If you retrace your steps, you will get to see the falls from a different perspective. Although none of these cascades are large, this mile-long section of Gill Brook is unusually waterfall rich.

The Gill Brook Trail, with a bypass to Indian Head overlooking Lower Ausable Lake, ultimately leads to a number of high peaks, including Nippletop, Dial, and Colvin.

FAIRY LADDER FALLS

Description: Further upstream, Gill Brook has produced yet another waterfall—90-foot, staircase-shaped Fairy Ladder Falls. It was at this waterfall in 1873 that the famous surveyor, Verplanck Colvin, his assistant, Mills Blake, botanist Charles Peck, and three guides including the legendary Old Mountain Phelps, camped before

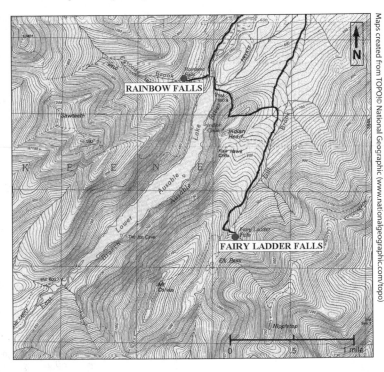

Maps created from TOPO!© National Geographic (www.nationalgeographic.com/topo)

ascending Mount Colvin and exploring Elk Pass. It was Colvin who named the falls. Colvin determined the elevation of the falls to be 3111 feet, nearly 0.6 mile above sea level. That makes Fairy Ladder Falls the highest major waterfall in the Adirondacks.

Directions: From Artists Falls continue hiking upstream along the Gill Brook Trail for another 1.5 miles or so, and then bushwhack to the left for roughly 0.2 mile with the sound of falling water guiding you to the falls. Look for herd paths to the falls. If you reach Elk Pass, you have gone too far.

EXITING THE HIKE

O nce you have reached the junction of the Gill Brook Trail and Lake Road, there are two options: for expediency, take Lake Road and travel northeast; for aesthetics, get back onto the East River Trail. Either way you will return to the gate and watchman's hut where your hike began. Follow the Ausable Club Road back to your car.

You will have been hiking now for 5 to 6 hours and covered at least 10 miles. In the process you have walked along both sides of the East Branch of the Ausable River and visited a number of various and interesting waterfalls that have formed on its tributaries. Mile for mile it is undoubtedly the best waterfall hike in the entire Adirondacks.

FALLS ALONG THE ADIRONDACK NORTHWAY

The Adirondack Northway (I-87) is a 175-mile-long superhighway created in 1967 to connect Albany, the heart of the Capital District, with the Canadian border and Montreal. Over 90 miles of the Northway pass through the Adirondacks. From 1966-1967 the Northway was voted the most scenic highway in North America.

Prior to the Northway, Route 9 was the principal highway between the Capital District and Montreal. Rt. 9 passes through every small village and town along the way, so through traffic has to contend with traffic lights, stop signs, and stop-and-go traffic. The Northway, with its speed limit of 65 miles per hour and multiple lanes for passing, has opened up the "Great North" to travelers and tourists in a way that was not possible before. Unfortunately, it also has meant the demise of many restaurants, motels, and shops along Rt. 9 who depended on the traffic that the Northway subsequently diverted.

The section of this superhighway that most interests waterfall enthusiasts extends from Keesville, near the terminus of the Ausable River, south to Saratoga Springs. The journey down the Northway includes many side ventures—Ausable Chasm in Keesville, Blue Ridge Road off Exit 29, and numerous stops along I-87 as you head south towards Saratoga Springs and the Capital Region. These stops include: Pottersville, at the south end of Schroon Lake, where Natural Stone Bridge & Caves is located; Lake George, with its small falls in Hague and its massive waterfall at Shelving Rock; and the Saratoga area, where a number of pretty waterfalls can be visited.

Several large waterfalls, including 190-foot-high O.K. Slip Falls near North River and Kanes Falls near Fort Ann, are on private lands and not accessible to the public.

ADIRONDACK
NORTHWAY

RAINBOW FALLS

Location: Keesville (border of Clinton & Essex counties)

Accessibility: Roadside

Description: Rainbow Falls (also known, historically, as Birmingham Falls) is an impressive waterfall formed on the Ausable River, a large stream that rises from two branches issuing from the High Peaks region of the Adirondack Mountains and flows into Lake Champlain north of Port Henry. Seneca Ray Stoddard in *The Adirondacks Illustrated* described the falls and the Ausable River:

Situated at the head of Ausable Chasm, Rainbow Falls is the most visited waterfall in the Adirondacks.

"The river flowing quietly from the south and west, passes Keesville, plunges over Alice Falls, square against a solid wall of rock, turns at right angles and, wheeling around in confused swirls, now right, now left, falls in a mass of foam over the rocks at Birmingham, then hurrying downward between towering cliffs and over rocks where the sun never shines, emerges from the gloom out into the glorious sunlight, and onward to mingle with the muddy waters of Lake Champlain."

The falls are located at Ausable Chasm, a popular tourist attraction, and are formed at the head of the chasm. The falls are over 70 feet high and consist of a double drop. According to Paul Jamieson & Donald Morris in *Adirondack Canoe Waters: North Flow*, "the Chasm is very different from the gorges of Hulls Falls on the East Branch and Wilmington Notch on the West Branch. The walls are more box-like: deeper and more nearly vertical or even overhanging."

Although Rainbow Falls has migrated a considerable distance upstream since the chasm first formed, this process is unlikely to continue into the future because of the presence of a power dam spanning the top of the falls. The dam prevents further upstream movement of the falls, thus, for better or worse, the length of Ausable Chasm is now determined by the hand of man.

Rainbow Falls is formed out of Potsdam sandstone, which is the oldest sedimentary rock in New York State.

History: Ausable Chasm has been a well known commercial attraction in the northeastern Adirondacks since 1870, featuring an unforgettable, self-guided tour through a section of the mile-and-a-half-long chasm with sheer walls rising 100 to 150 feet above the river bed. One also can take a boat ride for a short distance down a section of the chasm where no catwalks have been installed.

In 1996 Ausable Chasm was devastated twice in one year by record high flood waters that destroyed much of the infrastructure. The catwalks and walkways have been rebuilt since, but the tour through Ausable Chasm is now significantly different from the way it was conducted prior to the floods.

In the 1800s the falls were used to power sawmills and gristmills.

Keesville, where Ausable Chasm is located, was first known as Long Shoot, then Anderson Falls. According to William Gazda in *Place Names in New York*, it finally was named Keesville after its founder, William Keese.

Directions: From I-87 (the Adirondack Northway) get off at Exit 34 and follow Rt. 9 north into Keesville. Go through the village and continue northeast on Rt. 9 for 1.3 miles, and you will arrive at the parking area for Ausable Chasm. Don't worry about getting lost on the way; there are signs everywhere!

Walk across the high bridge spanning the Ausable River next to the parking area, and Rainbow Falls will be clearly visible upstream. Industrial buildings and ruins surround the falls.

Ausable Chasm is open from Memorial Day to Columbus Day.

FALLS AT WADHAMS

Location: Wadhams (Essex County)

Accessibility: Roadside

Description: The falls at Wadhams are formed on the Boquet River, a large stream that rises in the High Peaks and flows into Lake Champlain at Willsboro. The flume-like falls can be readily seen from the north side of the bridge. A dam is located at the top of the falls, and a factory is still operational on the southeast bank just downstream from the bridge.

History: The area has a long history of industrialization. The first gristmill at the falls was built in 1802 by Jesse Braman & Aaron Felt. The community at that time was called Braman's Mills. Previously it was known as Coat's Mills.

A forge was constructed in 1819; then another in 1825 by Barnabus Myrick. In 1825 a sawmill and gristmill also were established by General Luman Wadhams, and the name of the community changed to Wadhams Mills (eventually shortened to Wadhams). The last forge stopped operating in 1884; the last saw mill in 1947.

In 1904 the Wadhams Hydroelectric Plant was constructed. Its original purpose was to furnish power to the iron mines at Mineville. Later it became a power supplier to the town of Westport.

Directions: From the Adirondack Northway (I-87) get off at Exit 31 for Westport and Elizabethtown and go east on Rt. 9N. Immediately turn left onto Youngs Road (Rt. 59) and drive north-cast for several miles. At the end of the road, turn right onto Rt. 8. Within 0.1 mile you will come to Wadhams (junction of Rts. 8 & 22). The falls are directly to your left, upstream from the bridge spanning the Boquet at this junction.

FALLS ON HOISINGTON BROOK

Location: Westport (Essex County)

Accessibility: Near roadside; easy walk along well-constructed nature path

Difficulty Level: Easy

Description: This small waterfall is formed on Hoisington Brook, a small stream that rises in the hills west of Westport and flows into

Gentle, tiny cascades, like this one on Hoisington Brook, possess a unique charm.

Lake Champlain just downstream from the falls. Westport sits atop a natural terrace that encircles Lake Champlain's North West Bay.

The cascades consist of several ledges totaling 6 feet in height. A scenic footbridge crosses over the brook near the top of the falls.

Directions: From the Adirondack Northway (I-87) get off at Exit 31 for Westport and Elizabethtown and proceed southeast on Rt. 9N into the village of Westport. Right after you pass the intersection of Rts. 9N & 22, you will cross over a small stream in the middle of town. Immediately turn left and park in the area for Lee Park.

From here follow the nature pathway, which quickly crosses a footbridge over Hoisington Brook and then goes under the Rt. 22 bridge, continuing on the other side as it parallels the stream for a short distance.

BLUE RIDGE FALLS

Location: North Hudson (Essex County)

Accessibility: Roadside

Description: Blue Ridge Falls is formed on The Branch, a medium-sized stream that rises, in part, from Elk Lake and flows into Schroon River just southwest of North Hudson.

The falls consist of a number of little plunges and ledges with a total relief of 15-20 feet.

Directions: From I-87 (Adirondack Northway) get off at Exit 29 (Newcomb/North Hudson). Turn west onto Blue Ridge/Boreas Road and drive uphill, going west for 1.4 miles. The falls will be visible to your left just after you pass the Blue Ridge Falls Campsite on your right.

Stay on the road; the falls are on privately-owned land.

HANGING SPEAR FALLS

Location: Flowed Lands of the High Peaks (Essex County)

Accessibility: 5.0-mile hike (one way) with elevation gain

Difficulty Level: Difficult

Description: Hanging Spear Falls is formed on the Opalescent River, a sizable stream that rises from the northern slopes of Mt. Marcy and flows into the Hudson River south of Tahawus. The falls consist of a 75-foot-high cataract that plunges into a deep gorge.

Adirondack Mts., N.Y., Near Source of Hudson River, Tahawus.

Tahawus is one of four inroads into the interior of the Adirondacks, and the most direct route to Hanging Spear Falls.

An 1836 entry in the journal of William C. Redfield (in *Peaks and People of the Adirondacks*) describes a visit to the falls: "After a tiresome ascent of this kind we came, about mid-day, to a fall or cascade of about 75 feet into a gulf as precipitous and secluded as that of Niagara with walls of 100 to 150 feet in height." The fact that Niagara Falls is described as "secluded" illustrates just how much New York has changed since 1836!

Seneca Ray Stoddard in *The Adirondacks Illustrated* describes the Opalescent River as "the wildest gorge in the country, where for two miles the river foams and thunders over successive falls, one fully seventy feet in height, through rifts in solid rock, five hundred feet in depth and scarcely eight feet across at the top."

History: According to legend, Hanging Spear Falls was named by an early visitor who imagined that the rock at the top of the falls looked like a spearhead with the rest of the cataract resembling the long shank of a warrior's spear. Before then the waterfall was given the Seneca name *She-awi-en-dan-we* by Charles Fenno Hoffman, but this name never really took hold, probably because of its unwieldy length and difficult pronunciation.

The first recorded visit to the falls was in 1833 when David Henderson and Duncan McMartin hiked up to the waterfall while exploring the surrounding land for the Iron Mines at Tahawus.

Additional Points of Interest: On the way to Hanging Spear Falls, don't miss visiting Opalescent Falls, a 15-foot-high cascade formed on the Opalescent River roughly 0.3 mile upstream from Hanging Spear Falls.

Directions: From I-87 (the Adirondack Northway) get off at Exit 29 and drive west on Blue Ridge/Boreas Road (Rt. 2) for roughly 17 miles until you see the turnoff for Tahawus (Rt. 25) on your right. This will be approximately 1.6 miles before you reach the junction of Rts. 2 & 28N. Take Rt. 25 north and continue along a dirt road until you reach the parking area for hikers destined for the interior of the south-central Adirondacks.

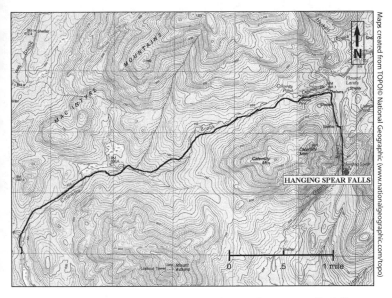

From the parking area, hike 4 miles northeast, initially follow-ing red-blazed markers, and then later, blue-blazed markers. The trail is easy to follow since it parallels Calamity Brook up to a hik-ing Mecca called The Flowed Lands. Along the way—at one mile from the trailhead—you will cross over a swinging bridge where a pretty, 4-foot waterfall can be seen. Near the set of lean-tos at the Flowed Lands, you will see a trail marker indicating a distance of 0.9 mile further ahead to Hanging Spear Falls. Follow the trail south, which is now red-blazed. You will notice that the lake slowly becomes narrower and more river-like at this point. At 0.4 mile you will reach the breached dam that at one time turned The Flowed Lands into a body of water much larger than the present one. Ford the stream directly above or below the dam and continue following the red-blazed trail as it proceeds downhill along the east bank of the stream. From here Hanging Spear Falls is only 0.5 mile away.

Along the way, within 0.2-0.3 mile a side path leads to Opalescent Falls, which is just off the trail and easily accessed. Between Opalescent Falls and Hanging Spear Falls is another large cascade, but it is hidden from view and located in a section of the gorge that is difficult to access.

In another 0.2-0.3 mile you will come to a side path on the right where a small sign points the way to Hanging Spear Falls. The cataract can be viewed from an impressive overlook along the rim of the gorge.

Further downstream, at the bottom of the gorge, a 10-foot-high cascade forms a natural barrier to entering the chasm.

SCHROON FALLS

Location: Schroon Falls (Essex County)

Accessibility: 0.05-mile hike (one way) from roadside

Difficulty level: Easy

Description: This tiny waterfall is formed on the Schroon River, a sizable stream that rises south of Euba Mills and flows into the Hudson River west of Warrensburg.

Despite the fact that this is not a big waterfall, the little gorge and slabs of horizontal bedding by the stream make an ideal place to have a picnic lunch or to just sit and contemplate how lucky we are that such places exist.

Directions: From the Adirondack Northway (I-87) get off at Exit 28 for Severance and Paradox Lake. From intersection of Rts. 74 & 9, go north on Rt. 9 for 2 miles until you come to Schroon Falls on your right.

Park at the northeastern end of the bridge, by River Road, and follow a pathway that leads down to slabs of bedrock next to the bridge.

FALLS AT NATURAL STONE BRIDGE & CAVES

Location: Pottersville (Warren County)

Accessibility: Self-guided walk along trails and across bedrock; some uneven terrain

Difficulty level: Easy

Description: The waterfall at Natural Stone Bridge & Caves is formed on Trout Brook, a medium-sized stream that rises in the hills north of Loch Muller and flows into the Schroon River by Pottersville. Trout Brook generally looks sedate during the tourist season, but in the early spring it can rise as high as 12 feet above its normal level as waters pour in from the watershed.

The waterfall consists of a broad, 8-foot-high cascade just a short distance upstream from the Natural Stone Bridge. It can best be viewed from Meditation Isle, where it is seen head-on. Side views are afforded at the old sawmill site and from along the Serenity Trail.

Natural Stone Bridge & Caves is a commercial attraction consisting of a gorge, a huge, natural stone bridge, and numerous caverns and potholes. One of the caverns, Noisy Cave, has a tiny waterfall of its own. The natural stone bridge is a great arch of rock with a span of 180 feet that looms 62 feet above the stream bed. In 1956 a block of stone estimated to weigh 9000 tons fell from the underside enlarging the aperture of the bridge and leaving a huge mound of rock deposited in the stream bed.

The Falls at Natural Stone Bridge at one time was harnessed for its
boundless energy.

An interesting phenomenon called Fiddlestring Falls can be seen from the Natural Stone Bridge overlook on Meditation Isle. Look to the left of the 9000-ton rock that fell from the stone bridge, and you will see a tiny string of water emerging from solid rock.

History: According to Clay Perry in *Underground Empire*, "at the waterfalls above the bridge are the remains of an old sawmill which was in working condition until forty-five years ago [i.e., 1902], at which time a huge dam was extended across the stream above the bridge to keep the logs from passing under it and getting into a jam." Clay Perry also describes Noisy Cave, where "four waterfalls cascade from high crevices."

A pamphlet from Natural Stone Bridge and Caves asserts, "The waterfalls of Trout Brook provided the water wheel power for early Dutch pioneers to cut lumber and grind grain (1750-1910). The old beam ... and some stonework are all that remain."

Directions: From the south take the Pottersville Exit (Exit 26) off I-87 (the Adirondack Northway) and turn left onto a road that takes you to Rt. 9 in 0.3 mile. Turn right onto Rt. 9 and drive northeast for 0.8 mile. Then turn left onto Natural Stone Bridge Road and drive northwest for 2.3 miles until you reach the parking area for Natural Stone Bridge & Caves.

From the north get off I-87 at Exit 26 for Pottersville, and immediately turn right onto Natural Stone Bridge Road. Drive northeast for 1.8 miles until you reach the parking area for Natural Stone Bridge & Caves.

Be sure to look for a tiny, manmade waterfall on your right 0.1 mile before the parking lot.

Natural Stone Bridge & Caves is open from late May to Columbus Day.

LAKE GEORGE REGION

"Black Mountain", 2665 feet above Sea Level. Highest Point on Lake George, N. Y.

Black Mountain at Lake George.

STAIR FALLS

Location: Crown Point (Essex County)

Accessibility: Roadside

Description: Stair Falls, also known as Staircase Falls, consists of a series of cascades and step-like ledges that are formed on Putnam Creek, a medium-sized stream that rises from Putnam Pond southwest of Chilson and flows into Lake Champlain at Crown Point.

The main waterfall is a drop of over 25 feet into a deeply-cut gorge. The other cascades are ledge falls varying from 2-4 feet in height.

Stair Falls is named for its series of step-like ledges.

Directions: From I-87 (the Adirondack Northway) get off at Exit 28 for Severance and Paradox Lake, and proceed east on Rt. 74. When you get to Rt. 22/9N, just north of Ticonderoga, turn left and follow Rt. 22/9N north for 2.1 miles. Turn left onto Rt. 7, which also is called Vineyard Road, and drive north for 4.4 miles. You will reach an intersection where you can only go left or right. At this point you will notice a medium-sized waterfall to your right just downstream from a bridge, and a small cascade just upstream from the same bridge. Drive straight ahead into a small parking area. Walk over to the bridge, from which you can view both falls.

Get back in your car, drive across the bridge and go east for less than 0.1 mile. Veer to your left and go up to Cross Road (Rt. 2). Turn left onto Cross Rd. and drive uphill for approximately 0.5 mile. Numerous stair-like falls will be visible on your left along Putnam Creek. The land is private and posted, but there are pull-offs where you can get out and look at the cascades from the road.

LACHUTE FALLS

Location: Ticonderoga (Essex County)

Accessibility: Near roadside; short walk over fairly level terrain

Difficulty Level: Easy

Description: Lachute Falls is located a short distance downstream from the outlet at Lake George's northern terminus. The falls are formed on a medium-sized stream that the French originally named Lachute River, and which later was changed to Ticonderoga Creek. Ticonderoga Creek is about 3 miles long and links Lake George and Lake Champlain. It drops a total of 230 feet as its waters flow from Lake George into Lake Champlain.

Lachute Falls—*la chute* is French for "the drop"—is roughly 30-40 feet in height, consisting of a long cascade followed by a 15-foot drop over a rocky bluff near the base. The fall's beauty is slightly marred by the cement foundation of an old building that straddles part of the top of the cascade. A large circular hole in the foundation serves as a conduit through which some of the stream passes. At the top of the falls are a great number of red bricks littering the creek bed behind the foundation. They are the ruins of a building that once stood at the fall's summit.

Further upstream is another falls where the stream bears to the left. The falls are 8-10 feet high and compressed on their northeast side by a brick wall. There is considerable evidence of past industry on both banks of the stream. Just above this falls, the stream ends at the foot of a small, 15-foot-high dam that holds back the waters of Lake George.

History: American Indians called this area *Chinandoga* (also spelled *Cheonderoga*), which means "place between two lakes" or "where the waters meet." Over time the name Chinandoga slowly transformed into Ticonderoga.

A "no man's land" of sorts once existed at the foot of the falls, which came to be known as Portage Landing. This no man's land divided the Iroquois to the south from the Algonquins to the north. War and hunting parties frequently would rest at the landing before continuing on their way.

Fort Ticonderoga nearby was originally known as Fort Carillon. *Carillon* is a French word that means "chimes." The eighteenth-century Frenchmen constructing the fort could hear in the distance the faint sound of Lachute Falls, whose cascades sounded like the tinkling of bells. The unusual monument at Moses Circle near the village of Ticonderoga was sculpted by Charles Keck. The four figures encircling the stone base depict a French soldier, an American Indian, a Highlander of the Black Watch, and a Green Mountain Boy.

There have been numerous mills on the stream since 1775 when the French first built a sawmill. By 1900 pulp and paper production had become the major enterprise of these mills.

Lachute Falls historically has posed a natural barrier for paddlers and boats navigating between Lake George and Lake Champlain.

Directions: From I-87 (the Adirondack Northway) get off at Exit 28 for Severance and Paradox Lake, and proceed east on Rt. 74 to the intersection of Rts. 74 & 9N. Turn right and drive south on Rt. 9N. As you approach the village of Ticonderoga, you will encounter a traffic circle (known as Moses Circle) with a large monument at its center. From the traffic circle proceed south on Lord Howe Street for 0.6 mile. Immediately after passing over a tiny rivulet that runs under the road, you will see a pull-off on the left side of the road. Park here.

You will see a sign stating, "Beware Water Rises Rapidly." (This is nothing you need to be concerned about during normal weather conditions.) A path leads directly from the road to the stream and the base of the falls.

To see the top of the falls, go back out to the road and walk up Lord Howe Street until you reach a second pull-off just around a sharp bend in the road. From there the top of the falls and the old cement foundations can be readily accessed.

If parking by the falls looks rutted and uninviting, drive back towards Moses Circle 0.25 mile and park in a public parking area where a historical maker provides information on the death of Lord Howe. From there simply walk back up the road the 0.25 mile to the falls.

Additional Points of Interest: Driving up to the top of Mt. Defiance makes for an interesting side trip. From Moses Circle drive east on Montcalm Street and then turn right onto Champlain Ave. Turn left onto The Portage (a one-way street) when the road forks. Turn left onto Mt. Defiance Road a short distance from this junction and follow it uphill to its end near the top of Mt. Defiance.

You will be rewarded with impressive views of the Champlain Valley. Mt. Defiance played an important role in the Revolutionary War. It was British General Burgoyne's threat of cannon fire from the summit of this mountain that forced the colonials' evacuation of Fort Ticonderoga in July 1777.

FALLS ON
HAGUE BROOK

Location: Hague (Warren County)

Accessibility: Upper falls, roadside
　　　　　　　　Lower falls, 0.05-mile walk (one-way)

Difficulty Level: Easy

Description: There are two sets of falls, 0.4 mile apart, formed on
Hague Brook, a small stream that rises on Ellis Mountain and flows

Millbrook Falls, Hague-on-Lake George, N.Y.

Hague Brook once provided sanctuary to salmon swimming upstream to
spawn.

into Lake George at Hague. The main (lower) fall is a 15-foot-high cascade visible from a pretty bluff that overlooks the stream. A path from the parking area runs through a grove of pines to a scenic overlook of the cascade where park benches provide for leisurely contemplation. The idyllic scene is marred only by proximity to Rt. 8.

The upper falls consist of one cascade and one flume, which are located on opposite sides of a small bridge crossing Hague Brook. The cascade, formed upstream from the bridge, is roughly 10 feet in height and located next to Green Acres by the Brook.

The cascading waters have carved out a deep chute, or fissure, just downstream from the bridge. The falls are so perfectly straight that one might be tempted to think that the sluiceway was manmade, but it is all natural.

History: It is hard to imagine today that Hague was once a land of tree stumps, having been stripped completely of its forests by lumber companies trying to meet the voracious demands of a growing America. The forests have grown back with a vengeance, and even Split Rock—an unusual rock formation that attracted thousands of tourists at one time—has disappeared into densely packed woods.

A number of rocks and boulders with large holes bored into them from the last glacier can be found at the edge of the lake near the village. Indians used them for cooking and for storing produce.

At one time New York State used this section of stream for harvesting eggs from landlocked salmon, which could swim no further upstream from Lake George than the base of the falls.

During the nineteenth-century age of industrialization, Hague Brook powered a number of mills along its banks.

George—the notorious Lake George sea monster—has Hague roots. The "monster" was created in 1906 by Harry Watrous, a well known painter, following a wager with Colonel W. D. Mann. Watrous fashioned his creature out of a pine log and painted it green with huge green eyes. A system of pulleys controlled secretly from shore enabled the monster to rise or submerge.

From the parking area for the lower fall, you will cross a cement bridge between two rock pillars. This road once led to a private residence that no longer exists except for sections of its foundations.

Directions: From I-87 (the Adirondack Northway) get off at Exit 25 for Brant Lake/Chestertown and proceed northeast on Rt. 8 for over 18 miles. About 0.5 mile from Rt. 8's intersection with Rt. 9N, you will glimpse the lower fall off to your right as you drive by (although it is not as easy to see if you approach from the west). Continue for about 100 feet past the fall and you will come to a parking area on the right.

From here walk over a small bridge, and then follow a short path for less than 0.05 mile up to a wonderful viewing area of the waterfall.

The upper falls can be viewed from roadside if you go 0.4 mile further northwest (uphill) on Rt. 8.

FALLS NEAR
CLAY MEADOW
TRAILHEAD

Location: Bolton Landing (Warren County)

Accessibility: 0.5-mile hike (one way)

Difficulty Level: Moderate

Description: This wispy cascade is formed on a small creek that flows down the mountainside into Northwest Bay Brook.

The cascade is roughly 20 feet high and should be seen in early spring or following a bout of heavy rain in order to view the falls at its optimum flow of water. The stream disappears into a ravine that goes off in a tangential direction from the main trail, thus making it easy for hikers to pass by without noticing that a waterfall is close at hand.

Directions: From I-87 (the Adirondack Northway) get off at Exit 22 for Diamond Point at Lake George, and drive north on Rt. 9N to Bolton Landing. Continue driving north on Rt. 9N for 6 miles from the second traffic light in the village of Bolton Landing. At this point you will cross Northwest Bay Brook. Proceed north on Rt. 9N for another 0.2 mile and park off to the right near the site of an old quarry that is now filled with water.

From the parking area walk back down the road going south for several hundred feet, and then pick up the trailhead for Clay Meadows just northeast of Northwest Bay Brook. Follow the wide Clay Meadows Trail downhill (east) and then over a wooden walkway where the trail crosses a swampy area. At 0.4 mile you will reach the

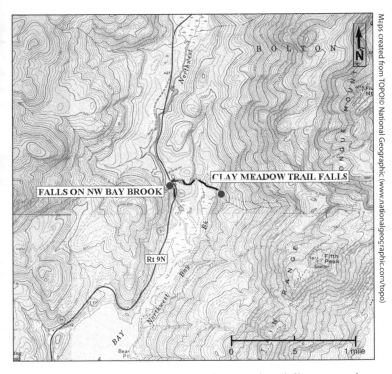

intersection of the main trail, which proceeds uphill (east) to the ridge between Fifth Peak and Five Mile Mountain, and the trail going off to the right (south) that continues to Tongue Mountain Point. Continue straight ahead on the main trail, going steadily uphill. Within 0.1 mile you will see a little path, easily missed, going off to the right that leads within 50 feet to a cliff overlooking the top of the falls.

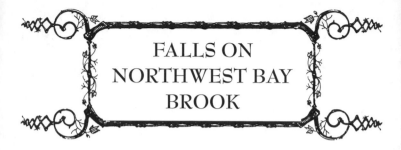

FALLS ON NORTHWEST BAY BROOK

Location: Near Bolton Landing (Warren County)

Accessibility: 0.1-mile hike (one way) over uneven terrain

Difficulty Level: Easy to Moderate

Description: These falls are formed on Northwest Bay Brook, a medium-sized stream that rises from Spectacle Ponds south of Swede Mountain and flows into Northwest Bay on Lake George.

The main waterfall is roughly 20 feet high and has formed at a point in the stream where Northwest Bay Brook makes a right-angle turn. The waterfall is bisected by a huge rocky buttress that forces the stream to fall to each of its sides. The smaller waterfall is downstream from the first and consists of a long, flume-like cascade approximately 8 feet in height.

Directions: From I-87 (the Adirondack Northway) get off at Exit 22 for Diamond Point at Lake George Village, and follow Rt. 9N north to Bolton Landing. From the second traffic light in Bolton Landing, at the center of town, drive north on Rt. 9N for about 6 miles. When you reach a small bridge that crosses Northwest Bay Brook, park at one of the several pull-offs on either side of the road. The gorge and falls are on the west side of the road.

The main trail follows the northern bank of the creek upstream from the bridge. This trail will lead you west up to the top of the gorge where you can see the main falls as you look down. On the way up you will pass a small cascade where the stream makes its first con-

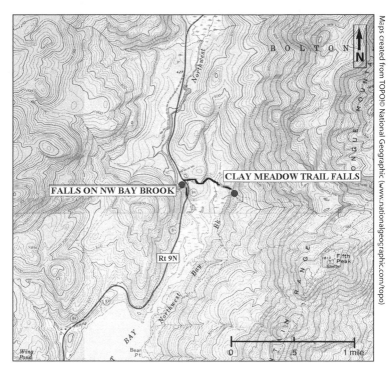

stricted right-angle turn. If you stand at this point, you will see the lower falls, which are only a short distance down from the main falls.

Although the well-worn pathway along the northern bank is obviously the trail of first choice for most hikers, the southern bank offers much better views for waterfall enthusiasts. From the southwest end of the bridge, follow a faint path leading down. The key to getting to the falls expeditiously is to hike up to the top of the escarpment (instead of following the stream bed), and then follow the faint pathway across the top of the escarpment until you reach the main falls. This vantage point will give you a head-on view.

SHELVING ROCK FALLS

Location: Shelving Rock (Washington County)

Accessibility: Less than 0.3-mile hike (one way) over fairly even terrain

Difficulty Level: Easy

Description: Shelving Rock Falls is a large waterfall, 70-80 feet high, formed on a medium-sized stream that rises near Buck and Erebus Mountains and flows into Lake George just downstream from the falls.

There is a dam at the top of the falls, but it is so small and unobtrusive that it is not offensive. The dam holds back a small amount of water, forming a pretty little pond.

An enormous pothole that has been carved out by swirling waters during times of high volume can be seen about halfway down from the top of the falls near the north bank. It resembles a large bathtub and probably has been used for a quick, cool dip by overheated hikers. Several large boulders rest at the bottom of the waterfall.

On the hike to the falls, a deeply cut gorge with a tiny stream at its bottom will be seen to the right. There are several, very small, dam-created falls on this creek, which enters the main stream a short distance below the base of Shelving Rock Falls.

History: According to the *Guide to Adirondack Trails: Eastern Region*, "Indian artifacts have been found in Shelving Rock Bay dating from 2500 B.C."

George Knapp, a vice-president of Union Carbide, built a grand summer home by Shelving Rock Mountain. A power house, once located at the base of the falls, served to generate electricity for the estate, including the railroad that traversed part of Knapp's property. In 1941 New York State was able to acquire a large chunk of this 20,550-acre estate.

Shelving Rock Falls is formed near the base of Shelving Rock Mountain.

Directions: From I-87 (the Adirondack Northway) get off at Exit 20 for Rt. 149, Fort Ann, and Whitehall, and proceed north on Rt. 9 for 0.5 mile. Turn right onto Rt. 149 and go east for 6.0 miles. Turn left onto Buttermilk Falls Road (yes, there is a Buttermilk Falls on this road, but it is on private property) and drive north. After several miles Sly Pond Road will enter from the right. Continue straight ahead. You will be on Sly Pond Road now. The land around you gradually will begin looking wilder and more remote, and the road will change from pavement to dirt. At 9 miles from Rt. 149, the road divides. If you look carefully, you will see an old, rusted sign stating "Shelving Rock Road." Take the left road at this fork and drive for another 0.8 mile. You will reach a parking area with trail signs reading: Black Mt. 4; Shelving Rock 4.4; Black

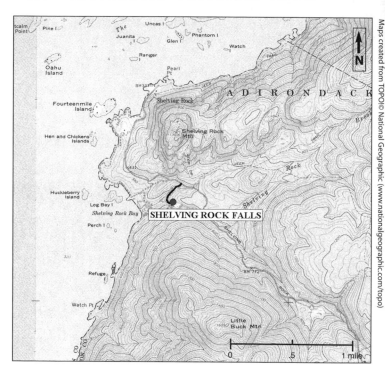

SHELVING ROCK FALLS

Mt. Pt. 7.8. Follow the road to the left, instead of driving into the parking lot, and proceed downhill for 2.7 miles. You will come to a small parking area on your right with a sign stating: Shelving Rock Mt. 1.7; Black Mt. Pt. 4.8. Pull in there.

From the parking area walk down the dirt road for another 100 feet and then follow an old four-wheel-drive trail that goes off to your left. Within less than 0.3 mile you will be at the top of the falls.

Exercise caution at the top of the falls and bear in mind the warnings voiced by the *Guide Adirondack Trails: Eastern Region*: "Many have been hurt here. The dam at the top of the falls is algae-covered and slippery." Don't add your name to the list of those who have been injured or killed.

Steep paths lead down the banks along both sides of the falls to the bottom. These paths should be attempted only by those who are surefooted and confident in their abilities.

Additional Points of Interest: For superb views of Lake George, it is well worth the time and effort to climb up to the 1130-foot summit of Shelving Rock Mountain. The trailhead begins from the same parking lot as for Shelving Rock Falls and is a hike of 1.7 miles (one way). The path (which is actually an old carriage road) leads to a series of ledges above the waters of Lake George at the head of the Narrows.

The cliffs at the top of the mountain are of significant interest to American literature. In James Fenimore Cooper's *The Last of the Mohicans*, Uncas, son of Chingachgook, a Mohican chief, is knifed by an enemy and his lifeless body is hurled from these cliffs, leaving Chingachgook alone as the last of the Mohicans.

For waterfall enthusiasts there is a long cascade in a deep gully that can be seen on the drive back from Shelving Rock Falls. From the parking area, start up the dirt road. If you look to your left at 1.2 miles, the 25-foot waterfall will be visible in the ravine.

CASCADE ON CRANE MOUNTAIN

Location: Crane Mountain (Warren County)

Accessibility: 1.3-mile hike (one way) with elevation gain

Difficulty Level: Moderate

Description: The cascade on Crane Mountain is formed at the outlet of Crane Mountain Pond and consists of a long descent over smooth bedrock. From Crane Mountain Pond the small stream makes its way down the mountain, entering a Precambrian marble cave system near the bottom, and eventually flowing into Mill Creek, north of Garnet Lake.

Crane Mountain is a fabulous hike in its own right, taking you to a dome of rocky granite rising 2,000 feet above the valley floor with rocky cliffs near the summit, a mountain pond for swimming and cooling off after a hot summer's hike, and a marble cave with crawls and waterfall drops for those who are experienced, well-equipped cavers. At one time Crane Mountain had a fire tower on its peak, but the tower was dismantled in the late 1980s.

Directions: From I-87 (the Adirondack Northway) take Exit 23 and proceed west to Rt. 9 just outside of Warrensburg. Turn right onto Rt. 9 and drive northwest for 0.8 mile, turning left onto Rt. 418. Proceed southwest for approximately 5 miles. When you get to a T-intersection after crossing the Hudson River, turn left onto River Road and then quickly right onto Athol Road. Proceed northwest for approximately 1 mile until you reach another T-intersec-

tion. Turn right and drive north for 0.9 mile. Then turn right onto
Glen-Athol Road, drive north for approximately 3 miles, and go left
onto Pleasant Valley Road where the road forks. Follow Pleasant
Valley Road for about 3.5 miles as it goes north and then west.
When you reach a T-intersection in Thurman, turn right on High
Road and drive northwest for about 1 mile. Turn left on Garnet
Lake Road and drive for 1.4 miles. You will see a dirt road on your
right. Follow this dirt road (Ski Hi Road) for 2 miles (be prepared
for some bumps) and it will lead you to the trailhead.

　　From the trailhead, instead of veering right and proceeding
north up the mountain, continue straight along the old Putnam
Farm Road and follow the trail as it proceeds northwest. Then go
north up the side of the mountain to Crane Mountain Pond.

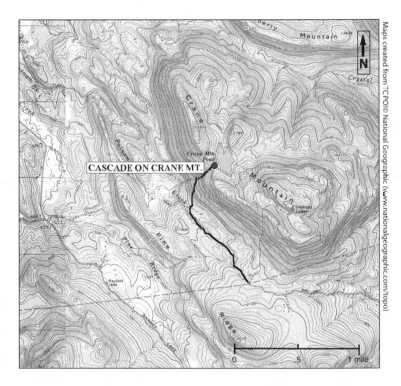

GLENS FALLS

Location: Glens Falls (Warren County)

Accessibility: Roadside

Description: The "Great Falls" at Glens Falls, now known simply as Glens Falls, is formed on the Hudson River. In *The Hudson River and its Tributaries*, Walter F. Burmeister states that the barrage and falls are 49 feet in height and describes the waterfall as "a gigantic honeycombed and terraced ledge." Benson J. Lossing in *The Hudson: From the Wilderness to the Sea* writes, "Glens Falls consist of a series of rapids and cascades, along a descent of about eighty feet, the water flowing over ragged masses of black marble, which here form the bed and banks of the river." Enormous potholes proliferate along the river bed.

Native American Indians called the falls *Chepontua*, meaning "difficult place to get around." This is just as true today, only now the falls—located at the head of a massive gorge—have sheer side walls that show the evidence of constant and unremitting industrial use over the past 200 years, with the gorge having undergone substantial modification of its natural structure.

James Fenimore Cooper immortalized the falls *In The Last of the Mohicans* when Hawkeye described it thus: "There are the falls on two sides of us, and the river above and below. If you had daylight, it would be worth the trouble to step up on the height of this rock, and look at the perversity of the water. It falls by no rule at all; sometimes it leaps, sometimes it tumbles; there it skips—here it shoots; hereabouts, it pitches into deep hollows, that rumble and quake the

Earth, and there away it ripples and sings like a brook, fashioning whirlpools and gullies in the old stone, as if 'twere no harder than trodden clay. The whole design of the river seems disconcerted. First, it runs smoothly, as if meaning to go down the descent as things were ordered; then it angles about and faces the shore; nor are there places wanting where it looks backward, as if unwilling to leave the wilderness to mingle with the salt!"

From the northeastern side of the bridge, you can see Cooper's Cave, also of *The Last of the Mohicans* fame. The cave is formed in the bedrock just downstream from the bridge. According to the March 2001 issue of *The Northeastern Caver*, "Until 1961, residents and tourists who went to the rocky river island could walk down to the cave using a spiral staircase from the bridge above. A combination of vandalism and disrepair led to the stairway's demolition in 1961, a year before a picture of the cave appeared in *National Geographic* magazine."

History: The falls were originally known as Wing Falls, after Abraham Wing, who came up from Dutchess County along with a number of other pioneers and founded a settlement of Friends & Quakers in 1763. The falls later became known as Glens Falls in

Glens Falls was made famous in James Fenimore Cooper's classic, *The Last of the Mohicans.*

honor of John Glen, Jr., from Schenectady, who acquired land in the area and built an early mill.

In past centuries the falls were considerably more powerful and energetic than they are today. In 1930 the Sacandaga River, a main tributary to the Hudson, was dammed to create a holding tank called the Sacandaga Reservoir (now known as the Great Sacandaga Lake), thus preventing spring floodwaters from tearing out bridges and flooding low-lying communities.

Directions: From I-87 (the Adirondack Northway) get off at the South Glens Falls Exit. Continue north on Rt. 9 for about 6 miles and you will reach South Glen Falls. When you come to a large bridge spanning the Hudson River and the gorge, connecting Glens Falls and South Glens Falls, pull over and park near the south end of the bridge.

The falls can be seen from the bridge directly upstream to your left. The view is marred, however, by having to look through a chain link fence.

ROCKWELL
FALLS

Location: Between Hadley & Lake Luzerne (Warren County)

Accessibility: Roadside

Description: Rockwell Falls is a pretty, eye-popping waterfall formed on the Hudson River just upstream from the Hudson's confluence with the Sacandaga River. The fall is roughly 10 feet high and horseshoe-shaped.

Lawrence I. Grinnell in *Canoeable Waterways of New York State* offers the following poetic description of the falls: "Just above the

Rockwell Falls is the Hudson River's most picturesque waterfall, located near the Hudson's confluence with the Sacandaga River.

bridge at Luzerne are raging falls preceded by heavy rapids ... which steepen and roughen, until they converge into a wild funnel, ending in a tumultuous falls."

Interestingly, the falls are not entirely natural. Robert M. Toole in *A Look at Metroland* writes, "originally a slight 12 feet wide, the walls were blasted out somewhat in order to build saw mills powered by the Hudson as it dashed through the narrow gap."

In *Rivers of Mountains* by Peter Lourie, John Bennett, a full-blooded Abenaki Indian who lives in the area of Luzerne near Potash Mountain, is quoted as saying that "Rockwell Falls is real dangerous right down in there. It's real deep, and you got a lot of current underneath that bridge." There have been a number of deaths at the falls. According to Bennett, a previous bridge was just dumped into the river along with an old cement mixer, creating much dangerous underwater debris for unwary divers and swimmers.

History: Rockwell Falls is named after Jeremy Rockwell, one of the original framers of the New York State Constitution. Rockwell operated the area's first sawmill on the west side of the falls.

American Indians called the falls *Boutakeese*. European settlers renamed it Little Falls, ostensibly to distinguish it from the Big Falls of Corinth. The *NYS Atlas & Gazetteer* lists the falls as Luzerne Falls.

In 1878 a dam was built at Rockwell Falls by Marcus Gardiner and Charles Rockwell.

The bridge spanning the Hudson River downstream from Rockwell Falls is called "The Bridge of Hope" and has had several incarnations. The original bridge, which was covered, existed until 1865. It was replaced by an iron bridge that was, in turn, replaced by a second iron bridge in 1930. By the late 1980s that bridge had become old and structurally suspect and was replaced in 1990 by the present bridge.

Additional Points of Interest: Hadley Mountain nearby is well worth a visit.

Whitewater rafting or tubing down the Sacandaga River is another consideration. There are several companies in the area that would be glad to help set up this adventure. For more specific information on whitewater tubing down the Sacandaga River, refer to this author's article, "Buoys of Summer," in the *1995 Annual Guide to the Adirondacks* published by *Adirondack Life* magazine.

Directions: From Saratoga Springs drive north on Rt. 9N passing through the village of Corinth. From the traffic light at the north end of Corinth, continue north on Rt. 9N for 4.5 miles until you reach the traffic light at the outskirts of Lake Luzerne. Turn left at the light onto Bay Road and continue along the edge of the Hudson River for 0.4 mile until you reach the center of the hamlet. Turn left onto Bridge Street (Rt. 4). Park on the side of the street and walk up to the bridge for excellent views of Rockwell Falls and the gorge.

MILL PARK FALLS

Location: Lake Luzerne (Warren County)

Accessibility: 50-foot walk (one-way) near roadside

Difficulty Level: Easy

Description: Mill Park Falls is formed on a tiny outlet creek that emanates from Lake Luzerne and flows into the Hudson River about 0.2 mile downstream from the falls.

The falls are no more than 25 feet high, altogether. The upper section consists of several ledges totaling 6-8 feet in height below a small dam just downstream from the Rt. 9N bridge at the outlet to Lake Luzerne. Directly below the footbridge is a small cascade. The main cascade is roughly 10 feet high and located slightly downstream from the metal footbridge over the creek, next to the building that houses the historical pulp mill machinery.

History: Benson J. Lossing in *The Hudson: From the Wilderness to the Sea* claims that the northern slope of Lake Luzerne, right at the fork of the Great Sacandaga and Oneida Trails, was an ancient gathering place for Indian councils.

In 1872 a German settler, Albrecht Pagenstecher, built a pulp mill next to the falls. Water was delivered to the mill from a stone dam on the creek via a long wooden conduit 3 feet in diameter. The dam still can be seen on top of the ledge falls.

According to Lester St. John Thomas in *Timber, Tannery, and Tourists*, the stream was also the site of a sawmill, gristmill, clothespin factory, tannery, a sash & blind factory, and several harness shops.

In 1936 the land was donated to the Town of Lake Luzerne by Pagenstecher's daughter, Helen Smidt, to be used as a park. In 1962 the Pulp Museum was opened to the public.

Directions: From the stoplight at the north end of Corinth, drive north on Rt. 9 for 4.5 miles until you reach the stoplight at the edge of Lake Luzerne village. Continue on Rt. 9 for 0.6 mile further. Turn left onto Mill Street, opposite Wayside Beach, and drive downhill for 100 feet. You will be across from Mill Park, on your left. Park off to the side of the street.

Mill Park Falls is a tiny waterfall on a once heavily industrialized stream.

BEAR SLIDE

Location: Near Lake Luzerne (Warren County)

Accessibility: 0.5-mile hike (one way) over uneven terrain

Difficulty Level: Easy

Description: Bear Slide (also known as Buttermilk Falls) is formed on Buttermilk Brook, a small stream that rises in the hills west of Gay Pond and flows into the Hudson River about 0.5 mile below the falls. The falls are located in the Hudson River Recreation Area.

The falls consist of a long slab of smooth bedrock some 100 feet in length, over which Buttermilk Brook glides for a total relief of roughly 50 feet. The slide ends with a plunge into a shallow pool of water. Local youths have used the huge slide for recreational pursuits, but not without some mishaps. According to Martin Rossoff in a pamphlet entitled "Annals of the Fourth Lake Community, Lake Luzerne," "Here [at Buttermilk Falls], sliding down the wet slopes resulted in shredded bathing suits and bare bottoms."

Directions: From Saratoga Springs take Rt. 9N north to Lake Luzerne. From Wayside Beach (on the lake), continue north on Rt. 9N for over 2 miles further until you pass Third Lake. Look for Gailey Hill Road on your left where a sign indicates the way to the Hudson River Recreation Area. Turn left onto Gailey Hill Road and follow it uphill (north) for 2.5 miles. When you reach Thomas Road, turn left and follow Thomas Road west for 0.8 mile. You will reach a dirt road, called River Road, that parallels the Hudson River.

Turn right onto River Road and drive north for about 1.3 miles until you reach the Hudson River Recreational Area. This is a good place to park because there are maps posted on an outdoor bulletin board.

From this point you can either drive or walk further north along River Road for another 0.2 mile. After you cross a small stream (Buttermilk Brook), follow a well-worn trail that leads off to your right going east into the woods. This trail will take you steeply uphill at first. Within 0.5 mile you will come to the base of Bear Slide

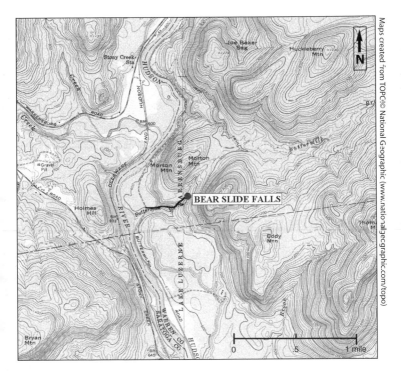

PALMER
FALLS

Location: Corinth (Saratoga County)

Accessibility: 0.3-mile walk (one-way) over old road

Difficulty Level: Easy

Description: Palmer Falls, also known as Jessup's Great Falls, is a 70-foot-high waterfall formed on the Hudson River.

The following description is taken from Nathaniel Bartlett Sylvester's *History of Saratoga County, New York*: "The river from

Palmer Falls is a prime example of what can happen to a picturesque waterfall if it is over-industrialized.

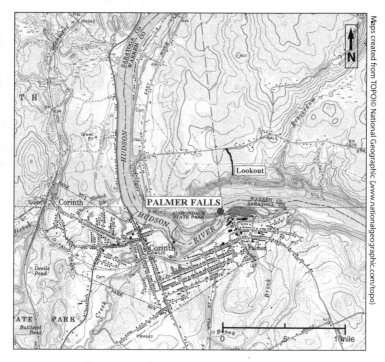

Jessup's Landing runs swiftly in a series of rapids between high banks until it reaches the falls. The southern bank is a sheer, rocky precipice about 120 feet high, fringed with pine, cedar, and hemlock at the top. The northern bank, though less abrupt, is a steep ascent, thickly wooded. The river bed is rocky and broken, and the waters of the river, for 50 rods above the falls, rush through a narrow channel descending some 30 feet in the distance, and hurl themselves over with irresistible force, dashing themselves to foam and spray as they descend the ragged, broken, and shelving rocks that form the face of the falls. The brink of the falls is in the shape of an arc, and in very low water can be crossed on feet dry-shod."

History: The land containing the falls was granted initially to Ebenezer Jessup, a pre-Revolutionary War settler. Later the falls became known as Palmer Falls because the land was owned by Beriah Palmer.

Directions: From Saratoga Springs take Rt. 9N to Corinth. At the end of town, by the northernmost stoplight, turn right onto East River Drive, crossing over the Hudson River. Curtis Falls (a dammed waterfall) is just downstream from this point. Proceed north for 0.7 mile and then turn right onto Call Street. Drive uphill (east) for 0.7 mile. You will see a sign stating, "Scenic Overlook." The overlook is maintained by the Curtis/Palmer Hydroelectric Company—a TransCanada project. Pull into a parking area on the right side of the road. According to the sign, the hiking trail is open sunrise to sunset from Memorial Day through Labor Day.

The hike to the overlook is an easy, 0.3-mile walk; be prepared, however, for a less than scenic view. The waterfall is dammed and heavily industrialized. Also be prepared for seeing only a nominal flow of water over the dam and falls because of the river being diverted for power generation.

FALLS ON SNOOK KILL

Location: Near Saratoga Springs (Saratoga County)

Accessibility: Roadside

Description: These pretty falls are formed on the Snook Kill, a medium-sized stream that rises in the hills west of Kings Station and eventually meanders into the Hudson River south of Fort Edwards.

The falls consist of a total drop of some 35-40 feet over a series of cascades, followed by a 20-foot plunge over a ledge-shaped block. The falls begin just below the Greenfield Road bridge at the point where it crosses the Snook Kill.

History: At the intersection of Parkhurst & Greenfield Road (less than 0.4 mile downhill from the falls) is a historical marker that reads, "Battle of Wilton. British forces of 250 whites and 240 Indians engaged French and Indian forces of 600 to 700 men."

Directions: From Saratoga Springs at the junction of Rts. 50 & 9, proceed north on Rt. 9. After 3 miles look for Worth Road on your right, and continue north on Rt. 9 for another 0.8 mile. Turn left onto Parkhurst Road (Rt. 36) and drive uphill for 0.3 mile. Turn left onto Greenfield Road (which ultimately leads to Greenfield Center) and drive uphill for 0.4 mile. Park to the side of the road when you reach Strakos Road, which comes in on your right. The falls will be directly to your left, easily visible from roadside.

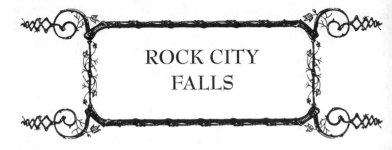

ROCK CITY FALLS

Location: Rock City Falls (Saratoga County)

Accessibility: Roadside

Description: Rock City Falls is formed on Kayaderosseras Creek, a medium-sized stream that rises south of Corinth and flows into Saratoga Lake opposite Cedar Bluffs. The falls are 10-15 feet in height and fairly broad.

History: At one time Rock City Falls was called "Big Falls," which is somewhat surprising considering its comparatively diminutive size.

The area has a long industrial history. In 1842 Rock City Mills was established at the falls. Several other factories, including Excelsior Mills and Empire Mills, were later established along the river. The present factory located at the falls is the Cottrell Paper Company. A trolley car line once ran over a small steel bridge that spanned the falls and a dam above the falls.

The village of Rock City Falls' main claim to fame is that it served as the summer home for industrialist George West, the man who invented the paper bag.

Additional Points of Interest: Several miles east of Rock City Falls is the famous Petrified Gardens, a commercial operation showcasing some of the finest displays of calcareous algaem (stromatolites) in the eastern United States.

Directions: From Saratoga Springs take Rt. 29 west. After passing through North Milton, you will arrive at the hamlet of Rock City Falls. You will see the Cottrell Paper Company on your left as you reach the outskirts of town. Turn left (south) onto Rt. 49, cross over a small bridge, and then park immediately on the right-hand side. The falls are directly upstream from the bridge and are visible from roadside.

Rock City Falls, another industrialized falls.

FALLS ON
MILL BRANCH

Location: Saratoga Lake (Saratoga County)

Accessibility: Roadside

Description: This small cascade is formed on Mill Branch, a small stream that rises from the hills above Saratoga Lake and enters the lake a short distance below the falls.

The waterfall is approximately 15 feet high and forms a long, descending cascade. At the top of the falls are the remnants of an old stone bridge that is slowly disintegrating. Only part of the bridge and several abutments remain standing. The stream passes through a tunnel and then spills over the top of the cascade.

Included in Frank Oppel's book, *New York: Tales of the Empire State*, are comments concerning Saratoga Lake and its tributaries:

"On its [Saratoga Lake's] eastern bank, steep declivities rise up from the water's edge, covered with tangled firs and hemlocks, some of which, the growth of centuries, rise above their fellows, 'till their tops, resembling so many spires, seem lost in the clouds. ... In the spring, considerable torrents pour down the deep ravines into the lake, forming cascades of some magnitude. One of these glens forms an echo almost as distinct and powerful as the celebrated one in the ruined bastion of the old French fortress at Crown Point. ... The Mohawks believed that the lake reflected their god's peaceful mind and that anyone crossing it would be drowned if he uttered a single sound."

One can only imagine what those Mohawks would think if they could visit Saratoga Lake in the twenty-first century!

The Indian name, *Saratoga,* has several possible derivations, according to Charles Albert Sleicher in *The Adirondacks: American Playground.* One is *Se-rach-ta-gue,* which means "the hillside country of the great river." A second possibility is *Sa-a-ta-ke,* or "the place where the track of the heel can be seen"—an allusion, apparently, to a nearby place where foot-like depressions can be found in the bedrock. A third possibility is that the word might mean "place of the swift waters."

Directions: From I-87 (the Adirondack Northway) get off at Exit 12 for Malta. Proceed east a short distance until you reach Rt. 9. Turn left onto Rt. 9 and drive north until you arrive at the turn-off for Rt. 9P. Turn right onto Rt. 9P and follow it around the southern end of Saratoga Lake. Eventually, you will come to Rt. 423, which goes off to your right. Continue straight on Rt. 9P past Rt. 423, and drive 1.2 miles north from this point. At an area called Maple Shade, turn right onto Brown Road. Within 0.2 mile Brown Road veers to the left, while another road goes to the right. The cascade is virtually at the point where the two roads meet, and can be seen from roadside.

The Falls on Mill Branch empty into Saratoga Lake.

ABOUT THE AUTHOR

Russell Dunn has written more books on waterfalls than any other author in the world and was profiled by the Associated Press in 2007 in a national feature article. His other works include: *Catskill Region Waterfall Guide: Cool Cascades of the Catskills & Shawangunks* (Black Dome Press, 2004); *Hudson Valley Waterfall Guide: From Saratoga and the Capital Region to the Highlands and Palisades* (Black Dome Press, 2005); *Mohawk Region Waterfall Guide: From the Capital District to Cooperstown and Syracuse* (Black Dome Press, 2007); and *Berkshire Region Waterfall Guide: Cool Cascades of the Berkshire & Taconic Mountains* (Black Dome Press, 2008).

Dunn is also coauthor with his wife, Barbara Delaney, of *Trails with Tales: History Hikes through the Capital Region, Saratoga, Berkshires, Catskills & Hudson Valley* (Black Dome Press, 2006) and *Adirondack Trails with Tales: History Hikes through the Adirondack Park and the Lake George, Lake Champlain & Mohawk Valley Regions* (Black Dome Press, 2009). His first book was *Adventures around the Great Sacandaga Lake* (Nicholas K. Burns Publishing, 2002). He is a frequent contributor of articles to regional magazines and newspapers including *Adirondack Life*, *Adirondac Magazine*, *Hudson Valley*, *Catskill Mountain Region Guide*, *Glens Falls Chronicle*, *Kaatskill Life*, *Northeastern Caver*, *Voice of the Valley*, *Sacandaga Times*, *Edinburg Newsletter*, and *Adirondack Sports & Fitness*.

Dunn is a New York State Licensed Guide. Together with his wife, Barbara Delaney (also a NYS Licensed Guide), he leads hikes to waterfalls in the Adirondacks, Catskills, and Hudson Valley, as well as to other areas of exceptional beauty and historical importance. Dunn is a popularizer of waterfalls and has given numerous lecture and slideshow presentations to regional historical societies, libraries, museums, civic groups, organizations, and hiking clubs. He can be contacted at rdunnwaterfalls@yahoo.com.

LIST OF WATERFALLS

ENDNOTES

Introduction

p. 15 Bruce Bolnick and Doreen Bolnick, *Waterfalls of the White Mountains* (Woodstock, Vt.: Backcountry Publications, 1990), p. 4.

p. 16 Scott A. Ensminger and Douglas K. Bassett, *A Waterfall Guide to Letchworth State Park* (Castile, N.Y.: Glen Iris Inn, 1991), p. 64.

p. 16 Rich Freeman and Sue Freeman, *200 Waterfalls in Central & Western New York: Finder's Guide* (Fisher, N.Y.: Footprint Press, 2002), p. 26.

Beecher Creek Falls

pp. 24-25 There is a picture of Beecher Creek Falls in *The Sacandaga Story: A Valley of Yesteryear* by Larry Hart (Schenectady, N.Y.: Larry Hart, 1967), p. 67.

West Stony Creek Falls

pp. 26-28 Almy Coggeshall and Anne Coggeshall, in *25 Ski Tours in the Adirondacks* (Somersworth, N.H.: New Hampshire Publishing Company, 1979), show a picture of the footbridge upstream from the falls in mid-winter, p. 58.

p. 26 Bruce Wadsworth, *Guide to Adirondack Trails: Northville-Placid Trail*, 2nd ed., edited by Neal S. Burdick (Glens Falls, N.Y.: The Adirondack Mountain Club, 1986), p. 58.

Tenant Creek Falls

pp. 32-34 According to Linda Laing, in *Guide to Adirondack Trails #7: Southern Region*, 2nd ed., edited by Neal S. Burdick (Glens Falls, N.Y.: Adirondack Mountain Club, 1994), "the waters are crystal clear and large rocks form a small natural amphitheater that invites a stop for rest and exploration," p. 87.

pp. 32-34 Barbara McMartin, in *Discover the Southeastern Adirondacks: Four-Season Adventures on Old Roads and Open Peaks* (Woodstock, Vt.: Backcountry Publications, 1986),states that "the falls are nearly fifty feet tall, a high slide of water over a sloping base with a dark hemlock frame," p. 38. A picture of Tenant Creek Falls is included on p. 37.

Falls on West Branch of the Sacandaga River

pp. 35-38 Bill Kozel, in "As Long as Rivers Run: Wet and Wild on the West Branch of the Sacandaga River," *Adirondack Life* XXV, no. 2 (March/April 1994), pp 41-73, describes a canoe trip down the West Branch and around the West Branch gorge.

pp. 35-38 Linda Laing, Tony Goodwin and Barbara McMartin, in "Glories of the Gorge," *Adirondack Life* XXIV, no. 6 (September/October 1993), pp. 40-45+, provide further information about the West Branch gorge.

Auger Falls

p. 41 Walter Burmeister, *The Hudson River and its Tributaries* (Oakton, Va.: Appalachian Books, 1974), p. 153.

pp. 41-43 There is a picture of the top of Auger Falls in *The Adirondacks: A Special World,* by Bill Healy (Utica, N.Y.: North Country Books, 1986), p.74.

p. 41 Bruce C. Wadsworth, *Guide to Adirondack Trails 3: Central Region,* 2nd ed., edited by Neal S. Burdick (Glens Falls, N.Y.: Adirondack Mountain Club, 1994), p. 133.

Austin Falls

pp. 44-45 A picture of Austin Falls in the winter can be seen in Barbara McMartin's *Discover the Adirondacks, 1* (Somersworth, N.H.: New Hampshire Publishing Company, 1979), p. 72.

p. 44 Wadsworth, *Guide to Adirondack Trails 3: Central Region*, pp. 133-134.

Squaw Brook Falls

pp. 50-51 Further information is contained in *Adirondack Profiles,* by William L. Wessels (Lake George, N.Y.: Adirondack Resorts Press, 1961), pp. 79-81.

Buttermilk Falls

pp. 54-56 Phil Brown, in *Longstreet Highroad Guide to the New York Adirondacks* (Atlanta: Longstreet Press, 1999), states that Buttermilk Falls is a "40 foot" spill over "a series of rock terraces on its way to Long Lake," p. 266.

pp. 54-56 Paul Jamieson and Donald Morris, in *Adirondack Canoe Waters: North Flow* (Glens Falls, N.Y.: Adirondack Mountain Club,1988), state that "Buttermilk Falls drops a total of 40 feet and is completely unrunnable. It is celebrated in Adirondack Murray's tall tale, 'Phantom Falls.' The falls is a popular picnic ground today with an impressive array of rock terraces leading to the shoreline," p. 72.

p. 55 S. R. Stoddard, *The Adirondacks Illustrated* (Albany, N.Y.: Weed, Parsons & Co., 1874), p. 104.

Bog River Falls

p. 57 Jamieson and Morris, *Adirondack Canoe Waters: North Flow*, p. 106.

p. 57 Stuart D. Ludlum, ed., *Exploring the Adirondack Mountains 100 Years Ago*, (Utica, N.Y.: Brodock & Ludlum Publications, 1972), p. 24.

p. 58 Mary MacKenzie, "Mystery at Bog River Falls," *Adirondack Life* IV, no. 3 (Summer, 1973), p. 10.

Griffin Falls

p. 63-64 Burmeister, in *The Hudson River and its Tributaries*, describes Griffin Falls as a "cataract formed by huge angular blocks of rock and ledges lodged between sheer cliffs" where "within 100 yards the stream bed drops 30 feet. ... Although the falls have only a 40 foot total drop, they are very impressive due to the formation of the narrow rocky chasm which funnels the waters over huge angular blocks of rocks and ledges." p. 98.

p. 63-64 A picture of the Griffin Gorge can be seen in Barbara McMartin's *Discover the Adirondacks, 1*, p. 27.

Shanty Brook Falls

p. 67-69 There is a picture of Shanty Brook Falls by John Baringer on the cover of *Adirondac* LII, no. 5 (June 1988).

p. 67-69 Bruce Wadsworth, in *Guide to Adirondack Trails 3: Central Region*, states that "The water of the falls tumbles over a 12 foot rock ledge into a deep pool below," p. 43. A picture of the waterfall is included on p. 130.

p. 68 Barbara McMartin, *Discover the South Central Adirondacks: Including the Siamese Pond Wilderness Area*, prepared with assistance of Dennis Conroy (Woodstock, Vt.: Backcountry Publications, 1986), p. 43.

Square Falls

p. 70 Burmeister, *The Hudson River and its Tributaries*, pp. 97-98.

p. 70 Barbara McMartin, *Discover the South Central Adirondacks*, p. 52.

p. 70-72 Bruce Wadsworth, in *Guide to Adirondack Trails 3: Central Region*, describes the falls as "quite broad. Water spills over the crest at several points, channeling into a deep pool at its base," p. 47.

Potholers

p. 78 Brown, *Longstreet Highroad Guide to the New York Adirondacks*, p. 181.

Monument Falls

p. 87 Bill Healy, *The High Peaks of Essex: The Adirondack Mountains of Orson Schofield Phelps* (Fleischmanns, N.Y.: Purple Mountain Press, 1992), p. 108.

pp. 86-87 Donald Morris, in "Canoeing the West Branch of the

Ausable: Jewel Among the Adirondack Rivers," *Adirondac* LIII, no. 3 (April 1989), describes Monument Falls as "a class III-IV drop of about eight feet," pp. 20-23.

High Falls Gorge

p. 88 C. R. Roseberry, *From Niagara to Montauk: The Scenic Pleasures of New York State* (Albany, N.Y.: State University of New York Press. 1982), pp. 163-166.

p. 90 Bradford B. Van Diver, *Rocks and Routes of the North Country, New York*, (Geneva, N.Y.: W. F. Humphrey Press, 1976), pp. 103-104.

Falls at Wilmington Notch Campgrounds

pp. 91-92 A picture of the Falls at Wilmington Notch Campgrounds can be seen on the cover of *Waterfalls of the Adirondacks & Catskills,* by Derek Doeffinger and Keith Boas (Ithaca, N.Y.: McBooks Press, 2000).

pp. 91-92 Morris, in "Canoeing the West Branch of the Ausable," states that "These falls drop about 60 feet in two distinct pitches," p. 23.

pp. 91-92 There is a picture of the falls in *State Parks and Campgrounds in Northern New York,* by John Scheib (Woodstock, Vt.: Backcountry Publications, 1987), on the reverse of the title page.

Flume Falls

p. 93 Donald Morris, "Canoeing the West Branch of the Ausable," *Adirondac* LII, no. 3 (April 1989), pp. 20-23.

p. 93 Stoddard, *The Adirondacks Illustrated*, p. 64.

Rocky Falls

pp. 98-99 There is an illustration of Rocky Falls in Elizabeth B. Jaffe and Howard W. Jaffe's *Geology of the Adirondack High Peaks* (Lake George, N.Y.: Adirondack Mountain Club, 1986), in which the fall is labeled a "diabase dike," p. 45.

p. 99 Jerome Wyckoff, *The Adirondack Landscape* (Gabriels, N.Y.: Adirondack Mountain Club, 1967), p. 19.

Indian Falls

p. 103 James Burnside, *Exploring the 46 Adirondack High Peaks* (Schenectady, N.Y.: High Peaks Press, 1996), p. 107.

p. 104 Edith Pilcher, *Up the Lake Road* (Keene Valley, N.Y.: Adirondack Mountain Reserve, 1987), p. 28.

p. 103 Sandra Weber, *Mount Marcy: The High Peak of New York* (Fleischmanns, N.Y.: Purple Mountain Press, 2001), p. 97.

p. 102-105 There is a picture of Indian Falls inside the front cover of

The Trails to Marcy, Recreation Circular 8, 1952, ed. (Albany, N.Y.: State of New York Conservation Department, 1920).

Falls on Tributary to Lake Colden

pp. 106-107 There is a photo of the falls, taken by Ed Sharp, in *Adirondack Life: 1991 Outdoor Guide* XXII, no. 4, p. 37.

Wanika Falls

pp. 109-110 A photo of Wanika Falls, taken by Jon Nedele, can be seen in *Adirondack Life: 1991 Outdoor Guide*, p. 41.

pp. 109-110 There is a photo of upper Wanika Falls in *Guide to Adirondack Trails: Northville-Placid Trail*, p. 42.

p. 109 Bruce Wadsworth, in *An Adirondack Sampler: Day Hikes for All Seasons*, 3rd ed. (Lake George, N.Y.: Adirondack Mountain Club, 1996), states that "Here, in a series of drops, water cascades several hundred feet to a pool," p. 92. A photo of part of Wanika Falls can be found on p. 91.

Cascade Lake Falls

pp. 111-112 Doeffinger and Boas, in *Waterfalls of the Adirondacks & Catskills*, state that Cascade Falls drops "down a hundred foot cliff," p. 28.

p. 111 Phil Gallos, *By Foot in the Adirondacks* (Saranac Lake, N.Y.: Adirondack Publishing Company, 1972), p. 17.

p. 112 Russell M. L. Carson, *Peaks and People of the Adirondacks* (Glens Falls, N.Y.: Adirondack Mountain Club, 1973), p. lxix.

Clifford Falls

p. 113 There is a picture of Clifford Falls in *The Adirondacks*, by Nathan Farb (New York: Rizzoli International Publications, 1985), pp. 44-45.

Falls on Tributary to Nichols Brook

pp. 114-115 Tony Goodwin's *Classic Adirondack Ski Tours* (Lake George, N.Y.: Adirondack Mountain Club, 1994) contains additional information on the Jack Rabbit Trail, p. 19.

Hulls Falls

pp. 116-117 In Elizabeth B. Jaffe and Howard W. Jaffe's *Geology of the Adirondack High Peaks*, the authors state that "The rocks range from granitic or syenitic gneisses without garnet to garnet-rich layers," p. 82.

pp. 116-117 A photo of the falls, incorrectly identified as on Halls Falls Road, can be found in *Upstate New York*, by Bradford B. Van Diver (Dubuque, Iowa: Kendall/Hunt Publishing Company, 1980), p. 37.

Falls at Jay

pp. 118-119 Wyckoff's *The Adirondack Landscape* contains a picture of Ausable River near Jay, showing how water has "sliced down into this dike of dark intrusive rock," p. 25.

Bushnell Falls

p. 120 Carson, *Peaks and People of the Adirondacks*, p. 155.

pp. 120-123 There is a photo of the waterfall in *The Adirondacks*, by Nathan Farb, p. 38.

p. 122 Pilcher, *Up the Lake Road*, p. 53.

Mossy Cascade Brook Falls

p. 124 Dennis Conroy, James C. Dawson and Barbara McMartin, *Discover the Northeastern Adirondacks: Four-Season Adventures from Lake Champlain to the Rock-Crowned Eastern Slopes* (Woodstock, Vt.: Backcountry Publications, 1987), p. 116.

pp. 124-127 In Elizabeth B. Jaffe and Howard W. Jaffe's *Geology of the Adirondack High Peaks*, the authors state that "In the ravine is a very shattered zone of rock, trending vertically and about NE ... which is probably the cause of the falls you see here," p. 91.

Roaring Brook Falls

p. 131 Burnside, *Exploring the 46 Adirondack High Peaks*, p. 49.

p. 131 Pilcher, *Up the Lake Road*, p. 82.

p. 131 Stoddard, *The Adirondacks Illustrated*, p. 139.

p. 131 Wallace Bruce, *The Hudson* (Boston: Houghton, Mifflin and Company, 1881), p. 202.

p. 131 John Winkler, *A Bushwhacker's View of the Adirondacks* (Utica, N.Y.: North Country Books, 1995), p. 56.

Falls on North Fork of the Boquet River #1

p. 135 Alec C. Proskin, *No Two Rivers Alike* (Fleischmanns, N.Y.: Purple Mountain Press, 1995), p. 70.

p. 135 Nathaniel Sylvester, *Historical Sketches of Northern New York and the Adirondack Wilderness* (Harrison, N.Y.: Harbor Hill Books, 1973), p. 96.

Falls on North Fork of the Boquet River #2

p. 136 A picture of the falls, taken by Ed Sharp, can be seen in *Adirondack Life: 1991 Outdoor Guide* XXII, p. 41.

East Branch of the Ausable River

pp. 140-163 Russell Dunn, "Hiking the Waterfall Trail," *Adirondac* LXII, no. 3 (May/June 1998), pp. 22-25.

p. 157 Laura Vicome, "Violence in the Valley," *Adirondack Waterways: 2001 Collectors Issue* XXII, no. 7, pp. 26-31.

Beaver Meadow Falls

pp. 150-152 There is a picture of Beaver Meadow Falls, taken by Albert Gates, on the cover of *Adirondack Life* XV, no. 5 (September/October 1984).

pp. 150-152 In *Guide to the Adirondack Trails: High Peaks Region*, 12th ed., edited by Tony Goodwin (Adirondack Mountain Club, 1992), Beaver Meadow Falls is described as a "falls of bridal veil-like appearance," p. 83.

Rainbow Falls (Ausable Lake)

pp. 153-156 Burnside, in *Exploring the 46 Adirondack High Peaks*, states that "Rainbow Falls shoots shimmering sprays 150 feet into narrow gorge," p. 145.

p. 155 *The Adirondack High Peaks and the Forty-Sixers*, edited by Grace Hudowalski (Albany, N.Y.: The Peters Print, 1970), p. 138.

pp. 153-156 Edith Pilcher, in *Up the Lake Road*, states that Rainbow Falls "plunges nearly 150 feet, bordered by dramatic rocky cliffs," p. 82.

p. 153 Clyde H. Smith, *The Adirondacks*, (New York: The Viking Press, 1976), p. 42.

p. 153 Stoddard, *The Adirondacks Illustrated*, p. 141.

pp. 153-156 There is a picture of Rainbow Falls in *Of the Summits, of the Forests*, edited by Tim Tefft (Morrisonville, N.Y.: Adirondack Forty-Sixers, 2001), p. 222.

p. 153 Wyckoff, *The Adrondack Landscape*, p. 35.

Artists Falls

pp. 158-160 A picture of the falls and flume on Gill Brook can be seen in *Up the Lake Road*, by Edith Pilcher, p. 83.

Fairy Ladder Falls

pp. 161-162 There is a photograph of Fairy Ladder Falls in *A Bushwhacker's View of the Adirondacks*, by John Winkler (Utica, N.Y.: North Country Books, 1995), p. 66.

Rainbow Falls (Ausable Chasm)

p. 169 William Gazda, *Place Names in New York* (Schenectady, N.Y.: Gazda Associates, 1997), p. 42.

p. 168 Paul Jamieson & Donald Morris, *Adirondack Canoe Waters: North Flow*, 3rd ed. revised 1994 (Lake George, N.Y.: Adirondack Mountain Club, 1988), p. 283.

p. 167 Stoddard, *The Adirondacks Illustrated*, p. 45.

Hanging Spear Falls

p. 176 Carson, *Peaks and People of the Adirondacks*, p. 41.

pp. 175-178 Pictures of Hanging Spear Falls and Opalescent Falls can be seen in *Discover the Adirondack High Peaks*, by Barbara McMartin (Canada Lake, N.Y.: Lake View Press, 1989), pp. 105, 107.

pp. 175-178 There is a picture of Hanging Spear Falls in *The Trails to Marcy*, p. 20.

p. 176 Stoddard, *The Adirondacks Illustrated*, p. 120.

Schroon Falls

p. 179 Lawrence Grinnell, in *Canoeable Waterways of New York State and Vicinity* (New York.: Pageant Press, 1956), states that "under the bridge is a shallow, rocky, 50-yard run which descends about 3 feet" (p. 215).

Falls at Natural Stone Bridge & Caves

p. 182 Clay Perry, *Underground Empire* (New York: Stephen Daye Press, 1948), pp. 36-42.

Falls on Hague Brook

pp. 189-191 A photo of the waterfall and chute can be found in *Guide to the Geology of the Lake George Region*, by D. H. Newland & Henry Vaughn (Albany, N.Y.: The University of the State of New York, 1942), p. 208. A photo of Split Rock can be seen on p. 215.

pp. 189-191 There is a picture of Hague Brook Falls in *New York Beautiful*, by Wallace Nutting (New York: Bonanza Books, 1927), p.125.

Shelving Rock Falls

pp. 196-199 James Fenimore Cooper, *The Last of the Mohicans* (New York: David McKay Company, 1973).

pp. 196,198 Carl Heilman II, *Guide to Adirondack Trails: Eastern Region*, 2nd ed. (Lake George, N.Y.: Adirondack Mountain Club, 1994), pp. 176, 178.

pp. 196-199 There is a picture of Shelving Rock Falls, taken by Jim Appleyard, on the cover of *Adirondac* L, no. 4 (May 1986).

Glens Falls

p. 202 Burmeister, *The Hudson River and its Tributaries*, p. 49.

p. 202 Cooper, *The Last of the Mohicans*.

pp. 202-204 Several photos of the falls and gorge taken in 1913 reveal the devastating power of the Hudson River. See Barney Fowler's *Adirondack Album, Volume Three* (Schenectady, N.Y., New York: Outdoor Associates, 1982), pp. 43-44.

p. 202 Benson J. Lossing, *The Hudson: From the Wilderness to the Sea* (Hensonville, N.Y.: Black Dome Press, 2000), p. 67.

p. 203 "Northeast News," *Northeastern Caver* XXXII, no.1 (March 2001), p. 5.

Rockwell Falls

pp. 205-207 Burmeister, in *The Hudson River and its Tributaries*, states that "Falls at Lake Luzerne consist of a constricted drop over one high and several lower steps totaling 9 feet," p. 31.

p. 207 Russell Dunn, "Buoys of Summer," *1995 Annual Guide to the Adirondacks: Great Outdoor* XXVI, no. 4, pp. 82-87.

p. 205 Grinnell, *Canoeable Waterways of New York State and Vicinity*, p. 133.

p. 206 Peter Lourie, *River of Mountains: A Canoe Journey down the Hudson* (Syracuse, N.Y.: Syracuse University Press, 1995), pp. 126-127.

pp. 205-207 There is a picture of Rockwell Falls on the cover of *Natural Areas of Saratoga County, New York*, by Claire K. Schmitt and Judith S. Wolk (Niskayuna, N.Y.: Environmental Clearing House of Schenecatdy, 1998).

p. 206 Robert M. Toole, *A Look at Metroland: A New Guide to Its History and Heritage* (Saratoga Springs, N.Y.: Office of R. M. Toole, 1976), p. 93.

pp. 205-207 There is a picture of a kayaker going over Rockwell Falls in "Going to X-Streams," *Adirondack Life* XX, no. 2 (March/April, 1989), p. 53.

Mill Park Falls

p. 208 Lossing, *The Hudson: From the Wilderness to the Sea*, p. 61.

p. 208 Lester St. John Thomas, *Timber, Tannery, and Tourists: Lake Luzerne, N.Y.* (Lake Luzerne, N.Y.: Committee on Publication of Local History, 1979), pp. 53-61.

Bear Slide

p. 210 Martin Rossoff, "Annals of the Fourth Lake Community, Lake Luzerne."

Palmer Falls

p. 212 Nathaniel Bartlett Sylvester, *History of Saratoga County, New York* (Philadelphia: Everts & Ensign, 1878), p. 391.

Falls on Mill Branch

p. 218 Frank Oppel, ed., *New York: Tales of the Empire State* (Secaucus, N.J.: Castle, 1988), pp. 141-142.

p. 219 Charles Albert Sleicher, *The Adirondacks: American Playground* (New York: Exposition Press, 1960), p 167.

BIBLIOGRAPHY

Adirondack Waterways: A Guide to Paddling the Northeast's Last Great Wilderness (supplement to *Adirondack Life*). West Chazy, N.Y.: Adirondack Regional Tourism Council.

Bolnick, Bruce and Doreen Bolnick. *Waterfalls of the White Mountains*. Woodstock, Vt.: Backcountry Publications, 1990.

Brown, Phil. *Longstreet Highroad Guide to the New York Adirondacks*. Atlanta: Longstreet Press, 1999.

Bruce, Wallace. *The Hudson: Three Centuries of History, Romance, and Invention*. Boston: Houghton, Mifflin and Company, 1881.

Burnside, James R. *Exploring the 46 Adirondack High Peaks*. Schenectady, N.Y.: High Peaks Press, 1996.

Burmeister, Walter F. *The Hudson River and its Tributaries*. Oakton, Va.: Appalachian Books, 1974.

Carson, Russell M. L. *Peaks and People of the Adirondacks*. Glens Falls, N.Y.: Adirondack Mountain Club, 1973.

Coggeshall, Almy and Anne Coggeshall. *25 Ski Tours in the Adirondacks*. Somersworth, N.H.: New Hampshire Publishing Company, 1979.

Conroy, Dennis, James C. Dawson and Barbara McMartin. *Discover the Northeastern Adirondacks: Four-Season Adventures from Lake Champlain to the Rock-Crowned Eastern Slopes*. Woodstock, Vt.: Backcountry Publications, 1987.

Cooper, James Fenimore. *The Last of the Mohicans*. New York: David McKay Company, 1973.

Cushing, Henry P. and R. Ruedemann. *Geology of Saratoga Springs and Vicinity*. New York State Museum Bulletin No. 169. Albany, N.Y.: The University of the State of New York, 1914.

Davis, Hamilton. "A River Rebounds." *Adirondack Life* XXXIV, no. 3 (May/June 2003).

Donaldson, Alfred L. *A History of the Adirondacks*. Vol I. Mamaroneck, N.Y.: Harbor Hill Books, 1977.

Doeffinger, Derek. *Waterfalls and Gorges of the Finger Lakes*. Ithaca, New York: McBooks Press, 1997.

Doeffinger, Derek and Keith Boas. *Waterfalls of the Adirondacks & Catskills*. Ithaca, N.Y.: McBooks Press, 2000.

Dunn, Russell. *Adventures around the Great Sacandaga Lake*. Utica, N.Y.: Nicholas K. Burns Publishing, 2002.

—"Buoys of Summer." *1995 Annual Guide to the Adirondacks: Great Outdoors* XXVI, no. 4: 82-87.

—"Hiking the Waterfall Trail." *Adirondac* LXII, no. 3 (May/June 1998): 22-25.

Ensminger, Scott A. and Douglas K. Bassett. *A Waterfall Guide to Letchworth State Park*. Castile, N.Y.: Glen Iris Inn, 1991.

Farb, Nathan. *The Adirondacks*. New York: Rizzoli International Publications, 1985.

The Forest Preserve of New York State. Compiled by Eleanor F. Brown for the Conservation Committee, Adirondack Mountain Club. Glens Falls, N.Y.: Schenectady Chapter of the ADK, 1985.

Folwell, Elizabeth. *The Adirondacks Book: A Complete Guide*. Lee, Mass.: Berkshire House Publishers, 2000.

Fowler, Barney. *Adirondack Album, Volume Three*. Schenectady, N.Y.: Outdoor Associates, 1982.

Freeman, Rich and Sue Freeman. 200 Waterfalls in Central & Western New York: Finder's Guide. Fisher, N.Y.: Footprint Press, 2002.

Gallos, Phil. *By Foot in the Adirondacks*. Saranac Lake, N.Y.: Adirondack Publishing Company, 1972.

Gates, William Preston, ed. *Turn-of-the-Century Scrapbook of Jonathan Streeter*. Glens Falls and Bolton, N.Y.: Gates Pub. Co., 1999.

Gazda, William. *Place Names in New York*. Schenectady, N.Y.: Gazda Associates, 1997.

Goodwin, Tony. *Classic Adirondack Ski Tours*. Lake George, N.Y.: Adirondack Mountain Club, 1994.

Grinnell, Lawrence. *Canoeable Waterways of New York State and Vicinity*. New York: Pageant Press, 1956.

Goodwin, Tony, ed. *Guide to Adirondack Trails: High Peaks Region*. 12th ed. Glens Falls, N.Y.: Adirondack Mountain Club, 1992.

A Guide to Long Lake and Raquette Lake. Long Lake, N.Y.: Economic Development Committee, Long Lake, 1985.

Hart, Larry. *The Sacandaga Story: A Valley of Yesteryear*. Schenectady, N.Y.: Larry Hart, 1967.

Healy, Bill. *The Adirondacks: A Special World*. Utica, N.Y.: North Country Books, 1986.

—*The High Peaks of Essex: The Adirondack Mountains of Orson Schofield Phelps*. Fleischmanns, N.Y.: Purple Mountain Press, 1992.

Heilman, Carl, II. *Guide to Adirondack Trails: Eastern Region*. 2nd ed. Lake George, N.Y.: Adirondack Mountain Club, 1994.

Heller, Murray. *Call Me Adirondack*. Saranac Lake, N.Y.: Chauncy Press, 1989.

Historic Edinburg. Edinburg, N.Y.: Town of Edinburg, 1992.

Hudowalski, Grace, ed. *The Adirondack High Peaks and the Forty-Sixers*. Albany, N.Y.: Peters Print, 1970.

Jaffe, Elizabeth B. and Howard W. Jaffe. *Geology of the Adirondack High Peaks*. Lake George, N.Y.: Adirondack Mountain Club, 1986.

Jamieson, Paul and Donald Morris. *Adirondack Canoe Waters: North Flow*, 3rd ed. Glens Falls, N.Y.: Adirondack Mountain Club, 1988.

Knight, Arthur, ed. *Adirondack Guide*. Lake George, N.Y.: Adirondack Resorts Press, 1950.

Kozel, Bill. "As Long as Rivers Run: Wet & Wild on the West Branch of the Sacandaga River." *Adirondack Life* XXV, no. 2 (March/April 1994): 41-73.

Laing, Linda. *Guide to Adirondack Trails #7: Southern Region*. 2nd ed. Edited by Neal S. Burdick. Glens Falls, N.Y.: Adirondack Mountain Club, 1994.

Laing, Linda, Tony Goodwin and Barbara McMartin. "Glories of the Gorge," *Adirondack Life* XXIV, no. 6 (September/October 1993).

Lord, Thomas Reeves. *Stories of Lake George Fact and Fancy*. Pemberton, N.J.: Pineland Press, 1987.

Lossing, Benson J. *The Hudson: From the Wilderness to the Sea*. Hensonville, N.Y.: Black Dome Press, 2000.

Lourie, Peter. *Rivers of Mountains: A Canoe Journey down the Hudson*. Syracuse, N.Y.: Syracuse University Press, 1995.

Ludlum, Stuart D. *Exploring the Adirondack Mountains 100 Years Ago*. Utica, N.Y.: Brodock & Ludlum Publications, 1972.

MacKenzie, Mary. "Mystery at Bog River Falls." *Adirondack Life* IV, no. 3 (Summer, 1973): 9-35.

McMartin, Barbara. *Discover the Adirondacks, 1*. Somersworth, N.H.: New Hampshire Publishing Company, 1979.

—*Discover the Adirondack High Peaks*. Canada Lake, N.Y.: Lake View Press, 1989.

—*Discover the South Central Adirondacks: Including the Siamese Pond Wilderness Area*. Prepared with the assistance of Dennis Conroy. Woodstock, Vt.: Backcountry Publications, 1986.

—*Discover the Southeastern Adirondacks: Four-Season Adventures on Old Roads and Open Peaks*. Prepared with the assistance of Willard Reed. Woodstock, Vt.: Backcountry Publications, 1986.

—*Discover the Southern Adirondacks*. Caroga Lake, N.Y.: Lake View Press, 1999.

—*Fifty Hikes in the Adirondacks: Short Walks, Day Trips, and Backpacks throughout the Park*. Woodstock, Vt.: Backcountry Publications, 1988.

—*Guide to the Eastern Adirondacks: Lake George, Pharoah Lake, & Beyond*. Glens Falls, N.Y.: Adirondack Mountain Club, 1981.

Minor, Jason. *Make a Splash: Swimming Holes and Waterfalls of the Green Mountains*. Swanton, Vt.: Master Studios.

Morris, Donald. "Canoeing the West Branch of the Ausable: Jewel among the Adirondack Rivers." *Adirondac* LIII, no. 3 (April 1989): 20-23.

Newland, D.H. and Henry Vaughn. *Guide to the Geology of the Lake George Region.* Albany, N.Y.: University of the State of New York, 1942.

"Northeast News," *Northeastern Caver.* XXXII, no. 1 (March 2001).

Nutting, Wallace. *New York Beautiful.* New York: Bonanza Books, 1927.

Oppel, Frank, ed. *New York: Tales of the Empire State.* Secaucus, N.J.: Castle, 1988.

Perry, Clay. *Underground Empire.* New York: Stephen Daye Press, 1948.

Pilcher, Edith. *Up the Lake Road.* Keene Valley, N.Y.: Adirondack Mountain Reserve, 1987.

Proskin, Alec C. *Adirondack Canoe Waters: South & West Flow.* Glens Falls, N.Y.: Adirondack Mountain Club, 1986.

—*No Two Rivers Alike.* Fleischmanns, N.Y.: Purple Mountain Press, 1995.

Reid, Max. *Lake George and Lake Champlain: The War Trail of the Mohawk and the Battle-Ground of France and England in their Contest for the Control of North America.* New York: Putnam's Sons, 1910.

Roseberry, C.R. *From Niagara to Montauk: The Scenic Pleasures of New York State.* Albany, N.Y.: State University of New York Press, 1982.

Rossoff, Martin. "Annals of the Fourth Lake Community, Lake Luzerne."

Scheib, John. *State Parks and Campgrounds in Northern New York.* Woodstock, Vt.: Backcountry Publications, 1987.

Schmitt, Claire K. and Judith S. Wolk. *Natural Areas of Saratoga County, New York.* Niskayuna, N.Y.: Environmental Clearinghouse of Schenectady, 1998.

Sleicher, Charles Albert. *The Adirondacks: American Playground.* New York: Exposition Press, 1960.

Sloan, Paul. *Lateral Thinking Puzzles.* New York: Sterling Publishing Co., 1991.

Smith, Clyde H. *The Adirondacks.* New York: The Viking Press, 1976.

St. John Thomas, Lester. *Timber, Tannery, and Tourists: Lake Luzerne, N.Y.* Lake Luzerne, N.Y.: Committee on Publication of Local History, 1979.

Stoddard, S. R. *The Adirondacks Illustrated.* Albany, N.Y.: Weed, Parsons & Co., 1874.

Sylvester, Nathaniel Bartlett. *Historical Sketches of Northern New York and the Adirondack Wilderness.* Harrison, N.Y.: Harbor Hill Books, 1973.

—*History of Saratoga County, New York.* Philadelphia: Everts & Ensign, 1878.

Tefft, Tim, ed. *Of the Summits, of the Forests.* Morrisonville, N.Y.: Adirondack Forty-Sixers, 2001.

Toole, Robert M. *A Look at Metroland: A New Guide to Its History and Heritage.* Saratoga Springs, N.Y.: Office of R. M. Toole, 1976.

The Trails to Marcy. Recreation Circular 8, 1952 ed. Albany, N.Y.: State of New York Conservation Department, 1920.

Van Diver, Bradford B. *Rocks and Routes of the North Country, New York.* Geneva, N.Y.: W. F. Humphrey Press, 1976.

——*Upstate New York.* Dubuque, Iowa: Kendall/Hunt Publishing Company, 1980.

Vicome, Laura. "Violence in the Valley." *Adirondack Waterways: 2001 Collectors Issue* XXII, no. 7, pp. 26-31.

Wadsworth, Bruce. *An Adirondack Sampler: Day Hikes for All Seasons.* Lake George, N.Y.: Adirondack Mountain Club, 1996.

——*Guide to Adirondack Trails: Northville-Placid Trail,* 2nd ed. Edited by Neal S. Burdick. Glens Falls, N.Y.: Adirondack Mountain Club, 1986.

——*Guide to Adirondack Trails 3: Central Region,* 2nd ed. Edited by Neal S. Burdick. Glens Falls, N.Y.: Adirondack Mountain Club, 1994.

Weber, Sandra. *Mount Marcy: The High Peak of New York.* Fleischmanns, N.Y.: Purple Mountain Press, 2001.

Wessels, William L. *Adirondack Profiles.* Lake George, N.Y.: Adirondack Resorts Press, 1961.

Winkler, John. *A Bushwhacker's View of the Adirondacks.* Utica, N.Y.: North Country Books, 1995.

Wuerthner, George. *The Adirondacks Forever Wild.* Helena, Mont.: American Geographic Publishing, 1988.

Wyckoff, Jerome. *The Adirondack Landscape.* Gabriels, N.Y.: Adirondack Mountain Club, 1967.

OUTDOOR TITLES FROM BLACK DOME PRESS

Catskill Peak Experiences

Mountaineering Tales of Endurance, Survival, Exploration & Adventure From the Catskill 3500 Club

Edited by Carol Stone White. 101 True Tales of High Adventure in the High Peaks. Paper, 6" x 9", 320 pages, map & photographs. ISBNs 9781883789596 / 1883789591 $19.95

Adirondack Trails with Tales

History Hikes through the Adirondack Park and Lake George, Lake Champlain and Mohawk Valley Regions

By Russell Dunn & Barbara Delaney. Paper, 6" x 9", 320 pages, maps & illustrations. ISBNs 9781883789640 / 1883789648 $17.95

Twenty-eight outdoor adventures to battle sites of the Revolution and French & Indian War, lost villages and resorts, great camps, old iron mines and tanneries, and trails made famous by Adirondack guides, artists, writers, and entrepreneurs.

A Kayaker's Guide to Lake Champlain

Exploring the New York, Vermont & Quebec Shores

By Catherine Frank and Margaret Holden. Paper, 6" x 9", 320 pages, photos, maps, original art. ISBNs 9781883789657 / 1883789656 $17.95

Every island, inlet, cove, and inch of shoreline the length and breadth of Lake Champlain—more than 650 miles in all—is explored in this treasury of information for kayakers.

The Adirondacks

By T. Morris Longstreth, introduction by Bill Ingersoll. Paper, 5.5" x 8", 390 pages, photos & maps. ISBNs 9781883789442 / 1883789443 $17.95

Reading it now, one can marvel at how different things are today, and, in some ways, how much better they are in the Adirondacks than they were eighty-eight years ago. Adirondac

A Kayaker's Guide to the Hudson River Valley

The Quieter Waters: Rivers, Creeks, Lakes & Ponds

By Shari Aber. Paper, 6" x 9", 224 pages, maps and photographs. ISBNs 9781883789534 / 1883789532 $16.95

www.blackdomepress.com   800-513-9013

OUTDOOR TITLES FROM BLACK DOME PRESS

Written in Stone

A Geological History of the Northeastern United States

By Chet Raymo & Maureen Raymo. Paper, 6" x 9", 176 pages, illustrations, graphs. ISBNs 9781883789275 / 1883789273 $16.95

Compresses billions of years into a slim, lively narrative.
Yankee magazine

Adirondack Peak Experiences

Mountaineering Adventures, Misadventures, and the Pursuit of "the 46"

Compiled & edited by Carol Stone White, foreword by Neil F. Woodworth, Executive Director, Adirondack Mountain Club, paper, 6" x 9", 320 pages, map & photographs. ISBNs 9781883789633 / 188378963X $17.95

Eighty-six true tales of adventures and misadventures in New York's Adirondack Park, written by more than 75 mountaineers including some of the most experienced backpackers in the Northeast.

Catskill Region Waterfall Guide

Cool Cascades of the Catskills & Shawangunks

By Russell Dunn, foreword by Edward G. Henry, Refuge Manager, US Fish & Wildlife Service. Paper, 4.5" x 7.5", 248 pages, maps, illustrations. ISBNs 9781883789435 / 1883789435 $14.95

This book is highly recommended for its unique combination of appealing writing, strong research, intriguing destinations, and interesting history. Kaatskill Life

Mohawk Region Waterfall Guide

From the Capital District to Cooperstown & Syracuse: The Mohawk and Schoharie Valleys, Helderbergs, and Leatherstocking Country

By Russell Dunn, foreword by Dr. Daniel A Driscoll, Chair of Land Preservation & Stewardship, Mohawk-Hudson Land Conservancy. Paper, 4.5" x 7.5", 336 pages, 90 illustrations & maps. ISBNs 9781883789541 / 1883789540 $15.95

Berkshire Region Waterfall Guide

Cool Cascades of the Berkshire & Taconic Mountains

By Russell Dunn. Paper, 4.5" x 7.5", 288 pages, 17 maps, 60 illustrations. ISBNs 9781883789602 / 1883789605 $15.95

OUTDOOR TITLES FROM BLACK DOME PRESS

Hudson Valley Waterfall Guide

From Saratoga and the Capital Region to the Highlands and Palisades

By Russell Dunn, foreword by Ned Sullivan, president,
Scenic Hudson. Paper, 4.5" x 7.5", 352 pages, maps & illustrations.
ISBNs 9781883789473 / 1883789478 $17.95

*Will very likely open eyes to a world of the outdoors that would have
passed us by otherwise.* Fred LeBrun, Times Union

Trails with Tales

**History Hikes through the Capital Region, Saratoga,Berkshires,
Catskills & Hudson Valley**

By Russell Dunn and Barbara Delaney, foreword by Karl Beard,
National Park Service. Paper, 6" x 9", 304 pages, illustrations,
80 photos,13 maps. ISBNs 9781883789480 / 1883789486 $17.95

This is a refreshing twist on the traditional guidebook. Adirondac

Catskill Trails Book One

A RANGER'S GUIDE TO THE HIGH PEAKSBook One: The Northern Catskills

By Edward G. Henry. Paper, 5" x 7", 184 pages, photos, maps, keys to
hikes. ISBNs 9781883789220 / 1883789222 $14.95

*Mr. Henry has tried to get us to slow down, smell the flowers, and appreciate
those "empty" miles between the trailhead and destination.* TrailWalker

Catskill Trails Book Two

A RANGER'S GUIDE TO THE HIGH PEAKS Book Two: The Central Catskills

By Edward G. Henry. Paper, 5" x 7", 184 pages, trail maps, photos,
keys to hikes. ISBNs 9781883789237 / 1883789230 $14.95

*So as you prepare for this season's Catskill hiking, I would add an
eleventh to Edward Henry's ten Hiking Rules and Guidelines: packand
use* Catskill Trails. New York State Conservationist

Berkshire & Taconic Trails

Massachusetts, Vermont and New York: The Ranger's Trail Guide Series

By Edward G. Henry. Paper, 5" x 7", 192 pages, maps, photographs,
GPScoordinates. ISBNs 9781883789565 / 1883789567 $14.95

*Serves as the perfect companion for Berkshire residents attempting to
trek some of the most daunting but rewarding hikes in all of New
England.* Berkshire Record

Rise and Fall of the Taconic Mountains

A Geological History of Eastern New York

By Donald W. Fisher, NYS Paleontologist Emeritus, in collaboration withStephen L. Nightingale, foreword by Dr. Robert Fakundiny, NYS Geologist Emeritus. Paper, 8" x 11", 192 pages, 140 maps, photos & illustrations, full-color fold-out map of the geological formations of Columbia County.ISBNs 9781883789527 / 1883789524 $24.95

Catskill Park

Inside the Blue Line: The Forest Preserve and Mountain Communities of America's First Wilderness

By Norman J. Van Valkenburgh & Christopher W. Olney. Featuring the photography of Thomas Teich, foreword by forest historian Dr. Michael Kudish. Paper, 8.5" x 11", 208 pages, maps, photos & illustrations, 32-page color section! ISBNs 9781883789428 / 1883789427 $21.95

Kaaterskill Clove

Where Nature Met Art

By Raymond Beecher, Greene County Historian. Paper, 8.5" x 10", 224 pages, maps, photos and illustrations. ISBNs 9781883789411 / 1883789419 $24.95

In their authoritative and well-researched volume, Van Valkenburgh and Olney have paid fitting tribute to an irreplaceable part of our national heritage. John Adams, National Resources Defense Council

American Wilderness

The Story of the Hudson River School of Painting

By Barbara Babcock Millhouse, foreword by Kevin Avery, The Metropolitan Museum of Art. Paper, 8.5" x 9.25", 208 pages, 64 illustrations (43 full-color paintings!). ISBNs 9781883789572 / 1883789575 $25.95

Books devoted to the Hudson River School today are legion, but none that I know quite performs the service that this one does, and so entertainingly. Kevin J. Avery, The Metropolitan Museum of Art